Psychological Wellness and Holistic Health Care

Psychological Wellness and Holistic Health Care

The Karmu System

Ricardo A. Frazer

Copyright © 2011 by Ricardo A. Frazer.

Cover Art: "Look To The East" (48" x 60") Oil painting by Ricardo Amando Frazer

ISBN:	Softcover	978-1-4568-1137-2
	Ebook	978-1-4568-1138-9

All rights reserved. No part of this book may be reproduced or transmitted in any form or by any means, electronic or mechanical, including photocopying, recording, or by any information storage and retrieval system, without permission in writing from the copyright owner.

This book was printed in the United States of America.

To order additional copies of this book, contact:
Xlibris Corporation
1-888-795-4274
www.Xlibris.com
Orders@Xlibris.com

Contents

Preamble 11
Forward 13

Chapter One: Introduction 15
Chapter Two: Psychological Theory and Practice 17
Chapter Three: Holistic Health Care 20
Chapter Four: The First Meeting 22
Chapter Five: The Second Meeting 28
Chapter Six: Another Day 34
Chapter Seven: My First Interview with Karmu 36
Chapter Eight: Dreams and More 38
Chapter Nine: Karmu on Joe Oteri Show, Boston,
                  with Compton O' Shaugnessy 44
Chapter Ten: Channeling Session with Karmu and Frida Waterhouse
                  On June 6, 1976 63
Chapter Eleven: Psychological Wellness 72
Chapter Twelve: The Crisis in American Health Care 82
Chapter Thirteen: Issues Relating Complementary and
                  Non-Allopathic Health Care in America 85
Chapter Fourteen: Silver Nanoparticles, HIV Treatment, and Uposh 89
Chapter Fifteen: Affirmative Acton Policy in
                  Medical School Admissions 96
Chapter Sixteen: Karmu's Healing Herbs and How to Use Them 105

Glossary 109
About the Author 111

This book is dedicated to Karmu. And to my Mother, Vera for supporting me and freeing me up to concentrate on my work. Special thanks to Enobong Esenyie for helping to type the manuscript and to Cynthia Wake for most gracious input.

"I am yesterday, today and tomorrow. I have the power to be born a second time. I am the source from which the gods arise."

—The Book of Coming Forth By Day

Look to the East was inspired by my relationship with Karmu. The title of the piece is a reference to Asia and Africa. The African mask and Asian symbols were integrated to depict Karmu's approach to cosmology, religion, and to healing all those who came for help. In the center of the piece is a literary character from Zen Buddhism. I thought of myself as this character—fishing for the truth but not empty handed.

Preamble

The Karmu Foundation was created to establish support for the work of Karmu. It was designed to provide funds and other things proper and necessary in furtherance of the creation of a universal spiritual community. It provided sustenance, shelter and clothing to those in need. It promoted universal peace and the study, practice and observance of spirit. This publication was completed in memory of Swami Muktananda Karmu as a tribute to the work he completed and to the greatness he achieved.

* * *

Forward

This writing is devoted to a discussion of the theoretical framework of Karmu's method of healing. My training is from several fields—intellectual and cultural history, political science, religion, psychology, and medicine. To these formal studies I have added the instructions of teachers from several living spiritual traditions (I have trained with Karmu for several millennia). From these many sources I have begun to synthesize an approach to healing which is flexible enough to accommodate the variety of ways in which illness and disease appears. In recent years such an approach has become known as holistic medicine.

Working with the whole person clearly entails attending to the physical, psychological, and spiritual dimensions of the human being. The socio-political environment must be incorporated simultaneously into the assessment of the cause and course of health and illness. Some people get lost in the wealth of detail involving such an endeavor because they fail to make use of plain old common sense.

Reliance on common sense is one of Karmu's fundamental principles. To take a typical question: what is the role of exercise in the healing process? One could elaborate on the fine points of increasing protective molecules (HDL—high density lipoproteins) in the prevention of coronary artery disease, heart attack and stroke. Yet we all have some sense, given the fact that much of the body is muscle, that stretching and working out maintains the body in optimal condition for daily function. This in turn helps set the proper environment for psychological balance and wellness. Karmu settled the question of exercise by working as a mechanic.

Ronald B. White, M.D.

Chapter One

Introduction

The Chief Executive Officer for the Immune Recovery Institute, Dr. Bradford, suggested to me that in the next twenty years we will see a transition in American health care whereby there will be other health care providers extending the work of the traditional medical doctor. There will be more non-physician health care extenders providing health care and operating outside of mainstream medicine. He suggested that one factor leading to this change is the need to reduce the financial burden of health care. This transition has been in motion for a long time, and I believe that Karmu and others like him are examples of this health care revolution. In time, the uneasy coexistence between traditional health care providers and those that complement the traditional mainstream system, will transform into greater compatibility.

Karmu, after a career as an automobile mechanic, became a healer who utilized a broad spectrum of natural techniques, including simple medicines, diet, fasting, massage, personal counseling, herbal, mineral, and externally-applied compounds to cure ailments. Numerous anecdotes, some garnered from Karmu himself, suggested that not only was he a healer, but also a priest, psychological counselor, political activist, mystic and sage. Like the indigenous shaman, Karmu mediated life and death through his ability to enter trance-like states. One of his gifts was the ability to alter the energy state of another person. He achieved this by his touch, by his presence, or through objects energized with his energy. Karmu stated that his practice was a combination of African and Asian healing techniques that he learned from his West Indian mother, his Ethiopian father, and other healers including Dr. Buzzard and Murshid Sam Lewis.

I was a Harvard University student studying counseling at the time I met Karmu, so I was fascinated with what I saw as an opportunity to gain further insight into the healing process and the process of change. The years I spent "at the feet" of Karmu left me inspired by his wisdom, compassion and courage. Karmu said he healed others by penetrating their subconscious to get in tuned with them. "Show them that they're loved, unconditionally and make them laugh," was his motto. Every visit with Karmu was a lesson in health, politics, and mysticism. I eventually completed the Karmu Foundation certification course in "Psychic, Herbal, and Alternative Healing" on July 19,1981.

I completed this course by visiting Karmu a couple days a week, starting in the fall of 1979. The other people visiting at the time were psychiatrists, nurses, ministers, drug addicts, alcoholics, lawyers, cab drivers, veterans of foreign wars, college students, and so on. In Karmu's words, there was never a dull moment. Some of the more well know visitors were people like Ram Dass, Malcolm X, Elijah Mohammed, Sufi Sam, David McClelland, and Alan Ginsberg, to name a few.

On many occasions, Karmu could be seen bringing himself and others to states of ecstasy through his "gift of gab" and his ability to provoke laughter and merriment. Frequently, he would appear to drop off into deep sleep, returning fresh with energy for another ritualistic episode, and speak of having left his body. This manuscript was endorsed by Karmu, and written in hopes of capturing some of the charisma, generosity, compassion and wisdom that was his. Related articles were included that reflect some of Karmu's medical interests. May his works continue to guide us.

Chapter Two

Psychological Theory and Practice

Swami Muktananda Karmu was born Edgar Warner in August, 1910. He transitioned in 1989. Karmu's system was constructed on a foundation of traditional Asian and African healing. He embodied a brand of psychology that was comprehensive, integrative, and incorporated the best practices of modern psychology. He synthesized some of the best theoretical insights of modern psychology into a practice that he used to guide and help legions of individuals struggling to overcome and deal with the hardships of modern living. This chapter is focused on the tenets of Karmu's psychological approach. Flowing through Karmu's practice are ideas articulated by Sigmund Freud, Carl Jung, Alfred Adler, and other central figures in the history of scientific psychology. Especially, Freud's psychoanalysis, Jung's analytical psychology and Adler's social interest.

Freud articulated a foundation for a scientific approach to understanding the unconscious mind. The unconscious was viewed as uncritical, programmable, and the reservoir of the individual's experiences. Dream interpretation was viewed as a way to access unconscious information. Insight was understood as a critical step towards changing unconscious programming. Hypnosis was viewed as a tool for enhancing individual recall of repressed and suppressed information, as well as a tool for changing existing programming, using suggestion.

Karmu employed all of these elements in his practice. He would let you know that he was penetrating your subconscious mind—I believe that he practiced a form of hypnosis in order to achieve this. One key to his hypnotic method was the way he modulated his speech patterns and tone. He spoke very fast, sometime very softly, and other times very slowly, in an intentional orchestration. Karmu often by-passed the conscious mind and subliminally imported suggestions into the person's subconscious, in order to alter the client's beliefs. If you didn't pay close attention, these techniques would go unnoticed. Karmu understood the power of belief in changing the structure of an individual's reality. He spoke of mind boggling things such as his visitations to a person while they were dreaming (e.g. catching them as they fell from a high cliff). The patient's conscious mind would be transported to a place where Karmu could speak directly to the divinity at the core of the individual's being. When Karmu spoke with conviction of things like his walking through walls, or walking on water, the conscious mind would be befuddled. The spiritual nature of the person was encouraged to drop all perception of inherent limitation. Karmu understood that spirit is limitless. The spirit of each person was directed to soar beyond the boundaries of physical limitation—a reminder of our true essence as spirits living a material existence. Karmu was a very fine hypnotist. Occasionally, he might even supplement these procedures with a few sips of an intoxicating, alcohol-based "red medicine"—an herbal preparation that reduced inhibitions and seemed to facilitate the hypnotic induction.

Karmu was highly intelligent even though he lacked formal academic training at the higher levels. He understood human nature, American society, and the multidimensional forces operating within the individual. Any open-minded person would grow in their insights about their self and the societal forces operating in their daily lives. These insights facilitated the growth of the individual's ego. In addition to treating the whole person, he fostered a sense of purpose, mission in life, and individual goals. Karmu directed each person to further develop innate potentials, to harness inherent abilities, and to effect change in the world. Each person was accepted and no one was rejected, regardless of station in life, life circumstances, or ability to pay. Karmu adapted himself to the needs of each person, and many of us were brought together to assist each other in our divine missions. He could see into each individual psyche and elevate our being, and our activity. He taught that each genuine spiritual tradition was valid and had the same ultimate goal of union with the divine. Spiritual and psychological growth was fostered through a merger of psychological and spiritual practice. He used his highly developed compassion and finely tuned empathic skills to model how we should be in the world. He taught that we should be loving, kind, respectful, compassionate and giving—he exemplified this behavior. Spiritual development was fostered pragmatically through practice, as well as reflection and conversation. He gave freely without expectation of return, thus creating an ascending vortex for change with himself at the center. His energy still vibrates and resonates in those of us who could see his value, and the blessings to be obtained through contact and connection with him.

Like Alfred Adler, Karmu used individual psychology as agency in social change. Karmu was deeply political and pressed others to understand the political system, the political forces in play, and social history. He was deeply sensitive regarding man's inhumanity towards others, and deeply committed to articulating these issues, regardless of how he was perceived. There were no sacred cows when it came to Karmu's political opinions. He said it the way he saw it, and pressed you to develop your social self, your social interest, and to become an agent for social change in your daily interactions. Like Adler, he understood that our long experience of dependency fostered an inferiority complex in each of us that was overcome thorough active social agency. As such, few healing session were complete without a lesson in current politics. He would call people out, and name names. No holds were barred, no villain unscathed, and certainly no blaming of the victim. He activated our moral compass and gave it direction.

Karmu's system of psychology was open, dynamic, and spiritual. It addressed body, mind, and soul. The conscious and unconscious minds were addressed as he helped us to develop a cosmic consciousness and to tap into the collective unconscious. We became more conscious of the God within. The God within us was activated through Karmu's journey into the cosmic arena. We became who we already were—cosmic beings of love and light on a divine mission to change the world.

Chapter Three

Holistic Health Care

Karmu's approach to physical health placed emphasis on diet, exercise, and detoxification. His approach to detoxification was fairly consistent, regardless of the ailment he was treating. All of his patients were instructed to detoxify using a solution of potassium permanganate that Karmu regulated. The chemical was said to be charged with Karmu's energy and he determined the concentration of the solution. As a patient, you were expected to bath in this blue solution and to do a warm water foot soak in the solution regularly. Potassium permanganate is legal chemical that can be bought through chemical supply companies. It's a strong oxidizer and is quite flammable. This chemical should not be mixed in any higher concentration than one that has the color of dark amethyst (1/4 tsp. per quart of water). Doses of 10 grams or so (a very, very large dose compared to Karmu's Blue medicine) can lead to poisoning, including fatal toxicity. Karmu regulated the dosage, keeping it at safe levels, and was highly adept in its use. However he is gone now, so those who use it medicinally should not use it as an eye bath since. It is damaging to eye tissue and can cause severe burning. Ingestion is also a highly questionable practice. It can cause severe burns to mucus membranes of the mouth, throat, esophagus, and stomach. When bathing in the solution, a cup or two with a couple tablespoons of sudsy ammonia is sufficient. When the water cools down it can be reheated and when the water changes color you have probably received the full benefit of the bath.

Karmu placed diet at the core of health care, however, dietary recommendations were individually-based and tailored to the specific health concerns of each person. Karmu stressed the eating of a balanced healthy diet including fruits, vegetables, proteins, grains and carbohydrates. He also stressed moderation in all things, and shunned extreme diets. He also recommended an occasional fast or break from eating. I was experimenting with vegetarian diets when I first visited Karmu, however, he suggested that I eat small to moderate amounts of meat. Then he got me into the habit of eating lots of soup—a practice that is still with me today.

He encouraged me to exercise as much as possible. He even taught me exercises he had developed for people who were confined to their bed. Massage was another real cornerstone in Karmu's protocol. He taught me his form of massage, using olive oil-based concoctions that he would put together and sometimes refer to as white medicine. He liked to assign colors to his medicines. For example, Black medicine was his general combination of herbs that would become Red medicine when brandy was added. As a result of Karmu's training, I became quite skillful at giving massages. Karmu also stress self-massage. His approach was of the deep-tissue variety that had to be done with a high level of skill and sensitivity. His approach included hand and foot reflexology, and required developing a great deal of bodily intuition. Under his tutelage your hands became skilled in where to go, and how much pressure to apply. A gentle tapping motion was his signature move. There was also a psychology underlying the massage that he taught, since massage was expected to bring up emotional pain and psychological content. There were many psychological dynamics to massage that Karmu passed on verbally. I felt that these teachings were at the core of his instructions.

Karmu worked on the physical and psychological level, but he also worked on the spiritual. While he seemed careful to teach no particular religious tradition, he taught a great deal of spiritually and encouraged you to learn from all religions. He said that all religions had the same source and the same goal. He would direct me to pay attention to things that were seemingly insignificant, like the meaning of a bird landing on his window sill. He encouraged me to pay attention to the type of bird and to assign a meaning to the birds appearance at that time—Karmu didn't believe in coincidence or accidents. He would also give you metal that had been in his presence for a period of time, or give you locks of his hair. These objects were said to have protective and beneficial properties. He also believed in clearing negative energy, and recommended substances for this purpose such as the burning of sulfur and salt together, the burning of sage, or the use of garlic and cloves. Karmu thought everyone could be psychic when they put their mind to it, practiced, and learned to shift their consciousness into very relaxed, receptive states, on command.

Chapter Four

The First Meeting

My first meeting with Swami Karmu was in the fall of 1979. I now suspect that our meeting was connected to a deep-seated need within me. A need I did not recognize at the time. Karmu and I lived about five city blocks apart from each other in Cambridge, Massachusetts. I was having severe muscle spasms in my lower back at the time and was deciding what to do about it. While walking down Massachusetts Avenue on my way to Harvard University, I saw a guy that I had met years before. We were undergraduates at the University of Connecticut. I told him about my back pain and he suggested that I see a local healer named Karmu. He was Latino and visiting a folk healer was a very natural thing for him, but I didn't have that mindset. The way I saw it, I was having a serious problem and needed medical attention, not a faith healer. I accepted Karmu's phone number, but I put it away with no real plan to use it.

Later that day, I made my way to the Harvard Medical Clinic and was told by a medical doctor to simply sleep on a firm surface. The doctor made no other recommendations. That night I found myself in excruciating pain and in a medical crisis. At about 3 am in the morning I got out of bed, fell to the floor, and could not get up. I laid there on my bedroom floor, in pain, unable to move, my housemate woke up about 4 hours later and heard me calling out in distress.

The police took me back to the same Harvard hospital I had visited earlier. I spent the next four days in a hospital bed taking various medications to control pain and relax muscles. When I was released from the hospital I was out of my pain crisis and I walked home in a drug stupor. Instead of excruciating pain,

I was experiencing dull but aching pain, along with brain fog. When I arrived home I located Karmu's phone number and gave him a phone call.

Ricardo: Hello, may I speak to Karmu?

Karmu: I'm Karmu, who's speaking.

Ricardo: My name is Ricardo. A friend of mine told me that you're a healer.

Karmu: How old are you, 28?

Ricardo: No, I'm 29.

Karmu: So I lie a little bit. I've been known to heal all diseases known to man. What can I do for you?

Ricardo: I've been having severe pain in my lower back, is that something that you deal with?

Karmu: We'll have you pain free over night.

Ricardo: That would really impress me.

Karmu: Why do you speak the Queens' English so well?

Ricardo: I'm a college student.

Karmu: Come right over, we'll have you running and jumping before you know it. You'll have zuk and wok, glide in your stride, and soon you'll be kicking Kung Fu like Fu Man Chu.

Ricardo: Do you mean come over right now and how did you know my age?

Karmu: I know things. Yeah, right now unless you're gonna be busy running track.

Ricardo: No, I'm not going to be running any time soon.

Karmu spoke fast and I was having trouble keeping up, but the warmth in his voice was palpable and welcoming. When he gave me his address I quickly realized I could be there in a matter of minutes. My head was still very foggy but I had no problem locating the house. The pain in my back was really saying something, "you're gonna be laying around the apartment for awhile, so don't make any plans. Reading and writing, no none of that either, I've got other plans for you. We're gonna sit and watch television. School work—forget about it. We're putting college on hold."

Karmu lived in a working class neighborhood, in a green house that he owned on Green Street. The street he lived on ran parallel to Massachusetts Avenue, one street over. The connecting street was Putnam Street. The embedded dirt and thick grime on the pavement made it apparent that Putnam Street was a high traffic area. It was daytime but the bar on the corner of Mass Ave and Putnam was in full swing. The door was open, I could see people inside. They were talking loud enough for me to make out conversations. Blues music was being playing on a jukebox. It seemed rowdy in there and the energy didn't strike me as friendly towards outsiders.

Karmu lived on the second floor of a two-level house right on the corner of Putnam Street and Green Street. The highly worn stairs up to the second floor creaked with anticipation as I walked up. If those stairs could talk, I'd hear all about an army of people who had beat them down. I was surprised to find that the door at the top of the stairs was unlocked, so I just walked in.

"Come on back here," A loud voice boomed out. "What took you so long?"

I was surprised to see a black man sitting on his bed as I walked into a small bedroom. I had not expected a member of my own race. His voice had not given away this part of his identity. A massive, shirt-less, Buddha-like figure was sitting on the edge of his bed with his feet on the floor watching television. He had big arms, powerful shoulders, large muscles, and a large belly. His hair was closely cut and some gray was cropping out on the sides.

He talked with his hands and smiled a lot. "You look like a movie star," he said. "No you look like nine movie stars. Soon, we'll have you glowing in the dark just like me. Here, take this bottle of blue medicine and go take a bath. When the bathwater gets cool, heat it up again. Soak for about an hour. There are paper towels in there you can use to dry off."

"He acts like he knows me," were my immediate thoughts.

The bedroom was not all that large and there was a bench across from Karmu's double bed. Over the head of the bed were a couple shelves. On one shelf was a turntable that wasn't hooked up to any stereo, on the other was a row of books. I could make out one of the book titles since I recognized it—"Memories, Dreams and Reflections" by Carl Jung. The room was fairly sparse. A bed, a dresser, a small refrigerator. A donation box shaped like a pyramid hung on the wall behind the bench. A few children's toys on the floor in the corner.

Karmu handed me a wine bottle with a purple liquid inside. He spoke quickly, and some of the words got by me, but I got the gist of his instructions and followed them. I thought to myself, "I don't even know him and he's letting me use his bathtub. Okay, why not, we'll give this a shot. He seems like a nice guy."

The bathroom was small and I was immediately struck by a large mural on the wall the tub was up against. It was a painting of a tree with lots of people coming out of it as if they were growing out of the tree. The mural was very colorful and organic—a picture I would characterize as "new age." It was an amazing image that I had not seen before. The artwork was striking, and extremely well done. I felt that someone had put lots of time and care into rendering it.

After an hour or so of soaking in the bathtub, I returned to the bedroom to find that a guy and a girl had arrived and were sitting talking. When I walked into to the room Karmu instructed me to remove my shirt and sit on his bed. He rubbed some liquid ointment in his hands and began to massage my neck and back while talking about the benefits of blue and white medicine. Blue medicine was a solution of potassium permanganate that I had soaked in, he said it would draw toxins out of my body. White medicine was a mixture of olive oil, peppermint, camphor, wintergreen, and other fragrant oils. Karmu talked as he massage my head, neck, and back. While he massaged he described what he was doing. He talked about manipulating my trigger points, stimulating my meridian system, energizing my chakras, and removing blockage in major energy centers, especially my neck. He tapped on some points and rubbed others, and inquired about the amount of pressure I was experiencing. While he massaged he explained that he was using personally designed techniques to free up my blocked energy, move the life-force around and activate more energy flow in my body.

Karmu: You're a bright guy, a golden child. I think I'll make you an SS, a special student. I hope you're taking notes cause we have a lot of ground to cover in a short amount of time. Right now I'm penetrating your subconscious with a DPE, a definite plus element, elevating your consciousness, and taking away your pain. I take your pain into my body, and disperse it out into the cosmic arena. It really hurts.

Ricardo: I don't think you want my pain.

Karmu: I can handle it, I handle it all. One week ago a woman arrived here all the way from Puerto Rico. She had a rare disease that no one could heal. She heard about me from healers on the island. They sent her to me. Her hands were cramped up for years. She was practically an invalid. I healed her in a week. It hurt me real bad. But I'm a bad dude. A dangerous cat. No pain can phase me. I'm up to the task.

I didn't know what to believe. Taking my pain into his body. Penetrating my subconscious. Dispersing pain into the cosmic arena. It all seemed pretty unbelievable to me.

Ricardo: How do you penetrate the subconscious mind?

Karmu: I get to know you. Who you are and how you think. I do it fast, real fast, you won't even know what's happening.

Ricardo: Well, I'd like to learn more about that. I'm studying psychology. Hypnosis is right up my alley.

Karmu: I knew we had a thinker here, come by often, as often as you like. I'll turn you into a T.C.—a topflight cat. You've got potential but your stiff, like a newly pressed shirt, we need to loosen you up.

  I didn't quite care for the reference to me as a stiff shirt. I was skeptical about Karmu as a healer, but I was eager to learn anything I could. The vibe coming from him felt genuine and caring. But a black healer—that was a first for me. Never mind a fast-talking black guy that wasn't making the kind of rational sense my university-trained mind was accustomed to hearing. The two other people in the room were paying attention to Karmu from time to time and at other times talking freely as if they were at home in their living room. Karmu continued to massage me and provide explanations of what he was doing. At times he would explain something to the people in the room or instruct them to eat some soup or drink some red medicine. Karmu was orchestrating the activity of everyone around him.
  After the massage I was instructed to soak my feet in a solution of hot water and blue medicine. I was told that this was another detox. Then I drank a solution of black medicine from a small paper cup. Karmu told me it was his special blend of herbs. Then I was given a bowl of hot vegetable soup that karmu said a chicken had been "dragged through"—there was a lot of onions and garlic in it. After eating I hung out for an hour or so. Karmu drank red medicine—his blend of wine, fruit juices and herbs, and offered it to other people who arrived. It didn't take long before there was a party atmosphere in the bedroom. The energy in the room kept getting higher and higher. Karmu laughed, joked, answered the phone, it was just crazy. I was mesmerized by all of what was going on and having fun at the same time. When I was ready

to leave karmu gave me a large brown bag filled with bottles of blue medicine and instructed me to bath regularly in the blue solution and to continue soaking my feet and drinking black medicine. We talked about the kind of foods I eat and he made recommendations. Then he told me what he usually charged for his services but commented that he knew I didn't have much money and that I could make whatever donation I felt I could handle. I found him to be gracious and extremely generous. I wasn't the kind of person who warmed up to people very quickly and I had just met Karmu, but already, I felt like a member of his family.

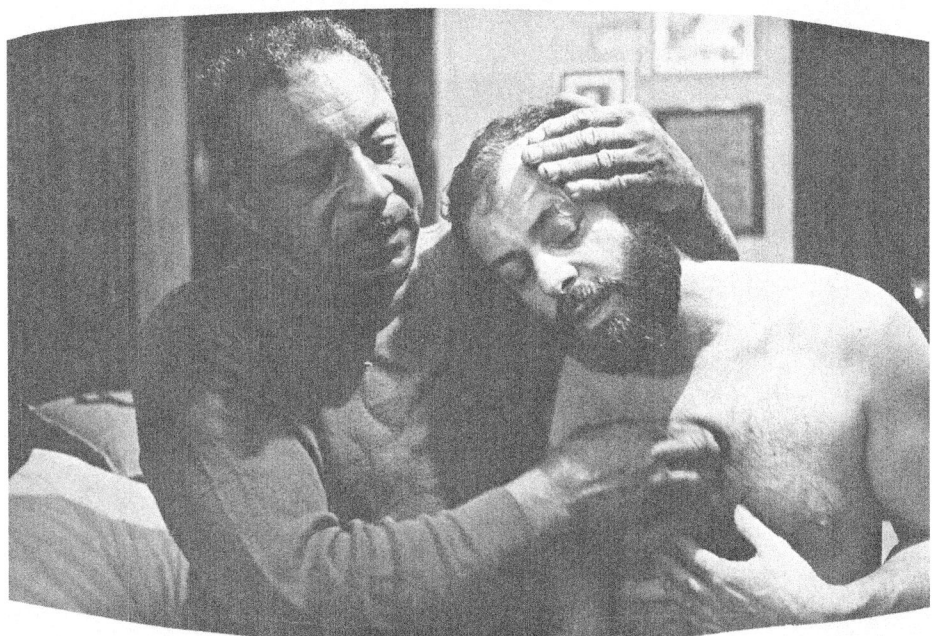

Chapter Five

The Second Meeting

The next day I woke up feeling like a million dollar man—pain free. I could hardly believe it. There was no fog in my brain and I felt like a new man. How did that happen? What did Karmu do to affect this change? I had been in excruciating pain, followed by extreme discomfort and a drug stupor. I expected to be miserable for a long time to come. The fog in my brain alone was depressing. Here I was, a high need-achiever in the middle of an academic semester and eager to get back to work, to compete and succeed. I definitely did not want to sit around taking prescription drugs. It was my first semester in college and my anxiety level was high. The anxiety alone may have helped trigger the muscle spasms in my back—I don't know. What I didn't expect was to get clear-headed and pain free in a day and be ready to get back to work. I had been told by my medical doctor to continue taking my medications daily for a month.

I went back to school that day. Some of my classmates had missed me and couldn't believe I had just spent four days in a hospital bed. So I offered to sell them my pain and muscle relaxing drugs, jokingly. They responded by razing me about trying to push drugs on campus. I was so amazed by how good I felt that I decided to get back to Karmu's house as soon as possible so I could begin to make sense out of the experience. Finding out how karmu healed people seemed just as important to me as master's degree study at Harvard University.

When I arrived back at Karmu's house a few days later, I met his live in assistant in the kitchen. I asked her if Karmu was in and she sent me to his room. She had been out of town, visiting her family, during my first visit. She was blond, with blue eyes—she was attractive and seemed socially withdrawn. She seemed friendly, but highly suspicious. I learn later from Karmu that she had had some bad experiences serving in the military. It was easy to tell that she took no B.S. from nobody. I didn't know who she was so I didn't say much and walked down the hallway to Karmu's bedroom.

"Look at you, walking straight and tall," said Karmu as I walked in the room. "You came in here like a wounded puppy, now you look like a dozen movie stars. How can we lose with the system we use. I knew you were coming by today. Take that bottle of medicine and take a blue medicine bath."

"I'm not sure I need it karmu," I said, "I'm feeling great."

"Well take one anyway," he said "I want you to fly high. You're a V.D.C., a very decent citizen."

"How did you know I was coming by karmu." I decided to follow up on his comment.

"Oh we know things around here," was his only reply. "Take a good hot bath but don't fill the tub to high. When you get straight A's at Harvard, you'll mention my name."

"Don't worry karmu," I said, "I've got your back. How did you know I went to Harvard?"

"Oh you've got questions, that's just what we like, but don't fret it lad, we do our homework around here too," he proclaimed. "When you finish your bath I've got something for you to read. I want you to tell me what you think."

After returning from my bath I received another back massage and drank some black medicine followed up with some red medicine. Then Karmu gave me a newspaper article to read. I was expecting to read something about psychology or health, instead the article was about Israel bombing a Palestinian settlement. When I finished reading I told Karmu that it was very complex politics that I didn't really understand but that I thought the conflict had ancient roots. I said it was a sibling rivalry between brothers that now hate each other. "Oh it's much more than that," he said. What followed was a long rant about the United States and the British creating a Jewish state, ousting Palestinian people and maintaining a military outpost in the Middle East. "How much do you know about these things," he asked. Not much I said, "I'm pretty naive about these issues." "Well I'll fill you in," he said. "You need to know these things. Forewarned is forearmed," He said. "Well fill me in" I said "I'm eager to learn as much as I can." "Have you read Howard Zinn" he said? "How about Noam Chomsky?" "I know of them, but no I have not read their work." "Well keep coming around, there's a lot you need to know. By the way, you should take my class it's called psychic, herbal and alternative healing. The cost is 250 dollars. You can pay in installments. Let me know when you're ready to start." "Sounds good to me Karmu, I'll let you know, when I'm ready." Then we both laughed. "You'll be a bad dude when you leave here, just like me, you'll be dangerous," He said. "I can go for dangerous, but we're not going to blow anything up are we?" I replied. "Oh you've got jokes too, I like that." "We're just trying to make people more aware of what's going on so things might get a little bit better in this country. Especially for the black man. It sure is rough out here for a black person."

Ricardo: You telling me!

Karmu: Just last week, one of my black patients lost his job because he married a white woman.

Ricardo: How do you know that was the reason, there are lots of reasons for getting fired?

Karmu: Oh his boss warned him not to do it. She was a pretty lass too. Beautiful, tall, great legs. They came by here and we talked about it. I warned them myself. White men don't want to see that. They get real jealous. In this country a black man is not supposed to be with a white woman. You can still get killed for that. But they were in love. I could see the trouble brewing. Now he's out of a job.

Ricardo: It's 1979 and that's still going on.

Karmu: Everywhere! North and South, East and West! Unless a black man wants to hold is head down, lay low and hide out, be better not get with a white woman.

Ricardo: How long has your lady friend been around Karmu?

Karmu: Oh she's been here a couple years. I helped her get back on her feet after the military abused her, then she started helping out around here. She remodeled this whole apartment, built the back room and repaired the back stairs. She's got excellent skills. I taught her how to get along with people. You should have seen her when she first came. She thought the FBI was trying to kill her. Now she's doing great and I can't get her to leave. I've told her she needs to move on so I think she's making plans. She's been mending things with her family lately.

Karmu: Have you seen your grandmother lately?

Ricardo: No I haven't seen her in years. She's an energetic ambitious woman but I don't think she's been doing too well lately.

Ricardo: Why did you bring up my grandmother?

Karmu: I've been picking up on her. How's her health been lately?

Ricardo: It hasn't been too good for years. She been dealing with diabetes most of her life. I don't really know how she'd doing, it's been a long time since I last saw her.

Karmu: Now may be the time. I've got a special clay-based poultice here. Have her use it on her feet. It was designed for horses but it works well on people. Look under my bed, there's a box of coins. Take one and keep it on you. If you don't find a coin take a safety pin. It doesn't matter, as long as it's metal. These metal pieces are collecting my vibration.

Ricardo: How will that help me Karmu?

Karmu: What matters is that it works. You want to keep my energy with you wherever you go. It will keep you safe and protect you. I'll give you some of my hair later. That works too. It's all about energy, mine is higher. When I was a baby my parents would use me to heal people. If someone was sick they would get to hold me for awhile. Their sickness would go away. I've known I had this ability all my life. When I was a young man I walked on water without falling in, it was a pond, I walked across it.

Ricardo: You walked on water? Karmu that violates the laws of physics. What did you have on my feet, Jets?

Karmu: No rubber boots. It was raining so I had my boots on. Many people saw it. I wasn't alone at the time.

Ricardo: I don't know anyone that can walk on water Karmu but I have heard about Jesus Christ.

Karmu: Well it was Christ-like. It's a gift. Did you eat yet? How about some soup it's good, real good. Onions, garlic, ginger, yams, the essence of Chicken. It's was made yesterday so it's had time to gel. Soup needs time to come together. It's like medicine when you make it right but it has to sit for awhile to come together. I make really good soup, well my people make it but now and then I have to re-train them. You hungry?

I didn't know what to make of what Karmu had said about walking on water. I was stunned and couldn't speak. I probably dropped into a hypnotic state. I suspected he sense it and continued on.

Karmu: Did you know I visit people in their dreams? I had a patient who was dealing with epilepsy. He was taking a whole shelf of medications. I changed his diet, put him on the proper foods, and took him off all his medication. I got him doing my exercises, and put him through my whole regimen. One night in his sleep he dreamed he was falling off a mountain. I came to him in his dream and caught him before he hit the ground. The next day he came to see me and told me about the dream. I told him I already knew about it. He never had another seizure.

I just sat there in Karmu's presence not knowing what to say. My eyes were probably pretty wide. I was trying to make some rational sense of it, but couldn't get my head around his statements.

Karmu: Did I tell you I walk through walls?"

At that moment a very exotic looking woman walked in the bedroom. She was very striking and had a look that I couldn't quite make out. She had soft straight hair that was parted in the middle and tied back in a bun. She looked part black, part white, part Native American. Her name was Diyanni. I was already in somewhat of a daze and now two highly spiritual people were laughing and having an unusual conversation that I could barely comprehend. So I just sat there feeling the vibe. I couldn't grasp most of the content. It was like being transported to another time and place. They talked about animals turning into people, people flying through the air like birds. I sat and listened for awhile, but I then got the feeling that this was a personal conversation, and that they needed space. Those thoughts entered my head in a vivid way. So I politely mentioned that I had work to do and needed to move on.

Chapter Six

Another Day

When I visited Karmu again he was on his bed, on his back, doing exercises.

Karmu: I work out every day. I do special exercises that I devised so you can exercise right in bed. I want you do learn them. This one is good for the stomach, abdomen and the low back. Lift your butt off the bed. Circle to the right five times, then circle to the left five times. Repeat that process 5 times. Make sure you get a good rhythm going with your breathing. Deep breathing from the stomach.

Ricardo: That looks pretty erotic karmu.

Karmu: Never mind that, it works. I've been doing these exercises my whole life. I'm as strong as an ox with great body tone. At 72 I'm still going strong. I last longer than most men. You need to do the one I just showed you. I recommend that you have a medical doctor check out your stomach. You've got something going on there. I'd also suggest that you get some colonics.

Ricardo: What's a colonic Karmu? I've never heard of that.

Karmu: It's a special kind of deep enema. Most disease begins in your colon. You can get a colonic at Ann Wigmore's center across the river in Boston. They'll turn you on to wheat grass. I don't use it but a lot of my patients have gotten great results with it.

Ricardo: What's blue medicine all about Karmu, I'd like to learn more about it.

Karmu: It's a chemical, potassium. It was used regularly in hospitals to disinfect surgical tools. Then the government had it taken off the market. I've heard it can be used to make explosives. That's how things work in this country. If it's cheap, readily available and effective the medical establishment will use the government to get rid of it. It's all about making money in this country.

At that point a very attractive middle age women knocked on the kitchen door and came into the bedroom.

"I really need your help Karmu," she seemed a bit frantic.

Karmu: Where have you been movie star. Didn't I tell you to come around more often. You look really really good. I should take you for myself. You were made for love. I rest my case. Golden boy, go up to corner and get me a quart of that high-grade brandy. I need it for my medicine.

Karmu located a few dollars and handed it to me. I suspected he was trying to get rid of me for a few minutes. I was happy to do the errand. Karmu was real generous with me so any opportunity to assist him felt like a blessing.

When I returned I learned that the women was married to a member of the mafia and that she had run away. She felt trapped and abused in the relationship, so she left but she was real scared and didn't know what to do. Apparently Karmu had interactions with the guy, and knew about his involvement with the mob. While I was gone, Karmu had managed to calm her down and alleviate some of her fears. I don't know what he did or what he said to her. Karmu seemed totally fearless. But a few other people walked in while she was there and since I was just hanging around she and I began to talk.

I found out that she was scared for her life and felt that she had to return to her husband. She told me that she had gotten with her husband when she was young and it took quite some time before she really knew what he did for a living. She felt there was nowhere she could go without being tracked down. So she was just going to wait it out for awhile and then return. I felt for her. I got the impression she valued having someone to talk too, so that's what I did, talk to her. I thought she was very attractive. Her hair was recently done, she was well manicured and she wore a mink coat. I got the impression that she had a comfortable life, materially, but didn't want that life anymore, because she lived in fear.

I started visiting Karmu about two times a week over the course of the next four or five years.

Chapter Seven

My First Interview with Karmu

Ricardo: You've stated that you can cure all ailments; do you still feel that way?

Karmu: Providing the patient has an open mind. Some people have built in prejudices. We had a case of a young man who was using shelves of medication. The first time he came here, all his ailments left. We gave him therapy and a short time later he came back and his ailments were gone. Therefore we conclude it was in his mind. If a person has an open mind we can heal almost anything.

Ricardo: How would you heal a child that had arthritis?

Karmu: We would immerse him in blue solution. Then we would manipulate his energy centers and talk to him in a positive manner; become him; talk to him in his own language. Therefore, you reach the mind and you reach the body.

Ricardo: How would you heal an adult that had back pains?

Karmu: There again you would penetrate his subconscious and free up his energy centers. Check his diet and see what he is taking wrong; give him the proper foods. Teach his friends to manipulate his energy centers, the coccyx, up and down the spine, and the rest of the body. We generally can heal back pains this way. Freeing up the nerve/energy centers is a key. In fact a blocked energy center in the neck stops the energy from going through. The result is the body does not function at full capacity. To give a person health you have to open up all his energy centers. That means going over the whole body.

Ricardo: So generally the approach is the same regardless of the ailment. Is that true?

Karmu: Unless the person is in a coma. In that case you manipulate the energy centers of their head. Their subconscious can accept information from your conscious mind even when the person is in a coma.

Ricardo: What's the source of your ability to heal?

Karmu: A lot of energy and the ability to act as a conductor of energy; cosmic energy from space. Also, an understanding of the human body and the ability to place myself inside the person's consciousness. I become them and I can feel their pain.

Chapter Eight

Dreams and More

Ricardo: Karmu, tell us about dreams. There seems to be a lot of mystery surrounding the topic on dreams. What is your understanding of dreams?

Karmu: When the conscious mind is at rest the subconscious mind brings up things that you would like to have happen or things you've seen in the past, or something you're going to see in the future. There are people who can look into themselves and define the dreams.

Ricardo: Identify the meaning?

Karmu: Right, I had a dream of meeting a person in a certain act at a certain time, three years ago. It actually happened. A woman passed me some pills from behind a bar. When it happened I told her about the dream.

Ricardo: So there's a certain predictive quality about certain dreams. One might be able to see into future occurrences.

Karmu: Positively.

Ricardo: What is man's purpose on Earth?

Karmu: To live in harmony with the Earth like the animals do. Not to spoil it but to keep it groomed. Understanding the Earth and being a part of it, as the trees are a part of the Earth. When a tree grows that is when it has its voice.

Ricardo: What does it mean to be part of the Earth?

Karmu: To be at one with the Earth.

Ricardo: Speak to us about peace, is peace among nations possible? Is world peace a possibility?

Karmu: Not as long as you have governments that stress individual grandeur and winner take all. That breeds jealousy and endless trouble.

Ricardo: Well the American government stresses individualism.

Karmu: It doesn't work. It causes the people to hate each other.

Ricardo: It pits one against another.

Karmu: Exactly, it doesn't work. It's better to have a social form of government where everybody helps everybody. If your boat is out of order everyone pitches in to help you repair it. It makes you feel good.

Ricardo: So you're talking about a place like Mexico.

Karmu: That's right, the black man who just ran for mayor of Boston lost the race because he pointed out that Fidel Castro does more good in the world than Ronald Reagan.

Ricardo: So you would say that Mel King's support of Castro had a negative impact on his candidacy?

Karmu: Definitely.

Ricardo: What were some other factors accounting for Mel King not showing as well as he thought he would?

Karmu: Well black people figured it would be a wasted vote; they don't believe in themselves. Like the black Banner editor who spoke harshly against King. Well it's time for the black man to start loving himself and start appreciating his culture. He's got a rich heritage, he built pyramids.

Ricardo: How ancient Africans constructed pyramids is still a mystery.

Karmu: There are glyphs inside the pyramids of people flying saucer crafts.

Ricardo: Do you think these are beings from another place or are these Earthlings?

Karmu: These are Earthlings who had a skill and a wisdom that has been lost.

Ricardo: Let's move to the matter of nuclear holocaust. Do you think nuclear holocaust is possible?

Karmu: Very possible.

Ricardo: How can we avert that?

Karmu: By taking the men who have gone mad out of office. The men who are so obsessed by their own power that they think we can afford to lose 5 million in a limited nuclear war.

Ricardo: The way to avert it is through the political process.

Karmu: Yes, getting them out of power is for the good of the people.

Ricardo: Change the power structure?

Karmu: Exactly.

Ricardo: How do we keep people in positions of power from becoming corrupted by their power?

Karmu: We need a governing board to keep those in power human.

Ricardo: Could you say a little more about how we keep politicians human.

Karmu: A coordinating board would only give the politicians a certain amount of money.

Ricardo: A ceiling on income level?

Karmu: It's a crime to give one man more money than he can spend.

Ricardo: I would like to speak to you about the Karmu Foundation. What is the present status of the foundation?

Karmu: It's lying in limbo with not too much happening. It's being talked about and people who want to support my healing work financially can do so, the way people support David Winfield's work with children.

Ricardo: What is a foundation?

Karmu: A foundation is a group of people who form with the aim of doing something for the public good in areas like education and health.

Ricardo: What is your vision associated with the establishment of a foundation?

Karmu: My vision is to get established in such a way that we're able to get funds to help young people become proud of who they are, so they can be of help to themselves, their people, and their government.

Ricardo: What do you plan to leave behind you as a lasting construction of your work?

Karmu: I intend to leave the medications I've used, like the herbs. I will leave my teachings of how to use the medications, and my teachings about diet. Additionally, there will be teachings about the problems associated with lying and hating, as well as my teachings on moderation.

Ricardo: Many have asked about what your donations are used for. Clearly you do not swim in luxury, but what does his income go towards. How do you respond to these inquiries about the aims towards which your funds are directed?

Karmu: They're directed towards staying alive and helping other people stay alive. Keeping down illness and disease is important. Right now I know a man trying to get 5 million to fight cancer. I need money in a similar way to instruct people, in simple ways, on how to take care of themselves naturally through nature's way.

Ricardo: Is the foundation being developed in any way?

Karmu: It's being discussed right now. We're getting people together who want to do something about it. We need personal help, coins are needed as well.

Ricardo: So is that how people who value your work contribute?

Karmu: If they want to help keep it going. For example I was on a boat where there was an out-break of a skin fungus and people couldn't keep their food down. We gave them all of the solutions I made up for them to wash their clothes in, wash their dishes in, and drink. In a short time the disease outbreak was gone.

Ricardo: So if people wanted to be a part of this work they could contribute their time, energy, and funds, is that correct?

Karmu: That is correct.

Ricardo: What is the relationship between your Church and your goals for a foundation?

Karmu: The same ideals, but they are separate because you can conduct a Church on a small scale. You take individuals who are sick and pray for them, and get them to pray for each other. You also teach them the skills for using herbs properly, proper exercise, and proper diet. From that they can improve themselves.

Ricardo: What programs do you see your foundation carrying out?

Karmu: Self-help and helping each other. A self-help center is where when you come broke, hungry and cold, funds are set up for you, and you're assigned a place to live and work. If later on you want to start a business you're loaned money at no interest.

Ricardo: This would be the function of the foundation?

Karmu: That's right, to help people help themselves.

Psychological Wellness and Holistic Health Care | 43

Chapter Nine

Karmu on Joe Oteri Show, Boston, with Compton O' Shaugnessy

Joe: Can you be cured of a disease by the laying on of hands? What is psychic healing? Here to tell us about it is a man known as Karmu who says he is a psychic healer who's cured thousands of people. With him is Compton O' Shaugnessy. What's a psychic healer, what do you do?

Karmu: Laying on of hands. We operate through prayer. We penetrate the subconscious and get in tuned with the person who is ailing.

Joe: Now you say you lay on hands, you pray, and you get in tuned with them. Are you basically saying that you can cure psychosomatic illness, but not real physical illness?

Karmu: We heal all ailments known to man.

Joe: All ailments, so it's more than just getting in tuned with the person, it's not just psychosomatic people you cure.

Karmu: That's right.

Joe: If I have a broken leg, the bone is sticking out one way and I'm laying there in agony can you lay your hand on me and cure my broken leg?

Karmu: We had a woman with a broken ankle, it had been so for a long time. We prayed for her, layed on hands, and penetrated her subconscious. We now have it written in my book that she walked six miles and danced all night the next day.

Joe: The next day! Had she been in a cast? Was she being treated by the standard physicians?

Karmu: For several weeks.

Joe: And she took the cast off and went dancing and walking the next day.

Karmu: That's right.

Joe: Did they later take x-rays to see if the bone had in fact healed?

Karmu: They did.

Joe: And it had?

Karmu: It had been healed.

Joe: That's pretty interesting. What kind of techniques do you use other than the laying on of hands, I know from looking at your book there are certain things you do. Why don't you tell the audience about them?

Karmu: We use diet, exercise, and herbal methods.

Joe: You mean if I have a poison in my system you could use a poultice of herb.

Karmu: We have a clay poultice with herbs, that could take care of it.

Joe: That takes care of it, so it's more than just psychic healing you also use. Besides the power of the mind, and prayer, you use natural substances like herbs and the rest of it.

Karmu: Natural substances that's correct.

Joe: So it's not just psychic healing, it's a whole range of things.

Karmu: That's right.

Joe: Compton you're a student of Karmu, what did you learn?

)ton: Well the most important thing I learned was to have a very positive attitude about what could happen and what I did in fact see happening in Karmu's house.

Joe: What did you see?

Compton: I saw people come in who would be very depressed, you talked first about emotional problems or psychosomatic illness, and a lot of people throughout the country are coming to realize that you can't really separate the physical and the emotional, there has to be a more holistic attitude towards health, and at Karmu's house the whole person is treated. Yes there's psychic healing that goes on, and like your question about if you had a broken leg, I would advise you to go to the hospital and get it set because that is something that modern medicine can deal with and can deal with very accurately.

Joe: Adequately.

Compton: Yes.

Joe: Well, you see the thing that I'm fascinated by is I believe that a lot of the illnesses that we suffer from, particularly in a high powered society like America are psychosomatic, there in your mind, they don't really exist but they're very painful to you. I can understand how your kind of treatment would help those people, but I have trouble bridging the gap with actual physical ailments, like the broken bone analogy.

Compton: Okay, I don't think the broken bone analogy is very good because that is something that can be so easily dealt with by standard medicine, but let's take a case of a person who has a disease like my mother had that could not be dealt with.

Joe: What did your mother have?

Compton: She was diagnosed with multiple sclerosis. She was in the hospital, the left side of her body was becoming paralyzed. It eventually became totally paralyzed within the space of three days, and I went to the hospital, and I saw her there, and I asked how she was being treated, and there was no treatment. There is no treatment for this disease, and they weren't doing anything for her, and I didn't know what to do, and I let my intuition take over and I said I've got to get her out of here. I brought her to my house and by using a combination of, as Karmu says; first aligning myself with her, allowing myself to you might say vibrate with her, laying on my hands, massaging her, loving her, hoping, praying for her that she would get well. I actually felt a negativity leave her body, and I knew at that exact moment it had happened, and I got her into bed. The next morning, I woke up to hear my mother in the front room walking and talking like normal and she hadn't been able to walk the day before.

Joe: That's amazing. Have you had any success treating people with cancer Karmu?

Karmu: Ninety percent.

Joe: Ninety percent cured!

Karmu: All over the world.

Joe: How do you know? Do you have any medical back-up?

Karmu: We do.

Joe: Really, what kind?

Karmu: Right now I'm working on a doctor from the Beth Israel Hospital in Brookline. He's diagnosed as having leukemia. After three visits I would say he's ninety percent healed.

Joe: You would say, but what does the medical profession say?

Karmu: They're about to take x-rays and confirm it.

Joe: Now, what kind of techniques, can you show the audience the techniques you use?

Karmu: Well, one technique would be to do the nerve centers, like so. This would be the third eye, a chakra. Free up all the nerve centers and give her the will. You penetrate her subsconscious with your mind, I'm an agent, I take the energy from the cosmic arena, penetrate her subsconscious with it, and she heals herself.

Joe: Where do your powers come from? Do you feel you've been selected by God? Do you see yourself as having special powers because I sure don't have that power. If I did that to her she'd punch me.

Karmu: I've got eight of my students healing cancer, all over the world.

Joe: You haven't answered my question, do you feel that God has singled you out.

Karmu: Definitely.

Joe: Now, you've told an interviewer that you walked on water?

Karmu: Yes, at nine years of age.

Joe: You actually walked across the swimming pool, or what-ever.

Karmu: No, I fell off a raft with a raincoat and rubber boots on. I couldn't swim.

Joe: And you walked across?

Karmu: Yes.

Joe: How far did you walk?

Karmu: Oh, I would say about ten yards.

Joe: As a result of that did you become aware of your special significance?

Karmu: I was born with it. I healed by my presence at three months of age.

Joe: By your presence?

Karmu: That's right. If you're sick and sit in front of me, you'll get better.

Joe: And that is backed up by medical science? Now, I don't want to be blasphemous, but the only other person I've read about who had this kind of thing was a man named Jesus.

Karmu: Read page 5 or 8 of the book

Compton: Well there is a testimonial about karmu, okay. Jesus was a person who transmitted healing energy. Also, to answer your question about selection, each individual has a talent they can do best. Now healing is definitely a talent, but everyone has the potential to be able to heal. What is happening when a mother puts her hand on the forehead of a child who is sick? She is in a way intuitively transmitting energy into that child and there are people who can learn to recognize the power in themselves, and learn how to develop it. Karmu happens to have been born with a great amount of vitality and what we call radiant white light that projects out to other people.

Joe: One thing I want you to answer for me, you also offer a number of services including cosmic cooking, flying lessons, and mating? Doesn't this somewhat demean your status as a chosen of God and a healer?

Karmu: It depends on how you take it. You need the proper foods to promote good health. We have herbal foods, we show you how to make them up.

Joe: I see, thank you very much.

KARMU SPEAKING AT THE BOSTON UNIVERSITY MEDICAL SCHOOL IN 1974

Karmu: We're here to discuss faith healing or healing with herbs. We use four methods. We use acupuncture, hypnosis, music therapy, and we invade the subconscious. We get very good results. It doesn't matter what they have, we get about a 97 percent success rate. We give herbs which purge the system, and then massage. Sometimes the person is healed in five minutes, sometimes three months. We just had a case about two weeks ago where a lady had cancer of the fallopian tube and she was supposed to have a hysterectomy. We gave her twenty hours of therapy and she never had the operation. If there are any questions, I'll be glad to answer them. Questions about the methods we use: when, why, and what for.

Questioner: Could you talk about herbs?

Karmu: Yes, we use a number of herbs from Africa and the West Indies. I'll name some; bitter aloes, we use goldenseal, Garfield tea, root of the cassava weed, and a number of others.

Questioner: Can they be grown locally?

Karmu: Yes, they can be grown here. In fact, I've grown some in my back yard in Alston.

Questioner: Are these all for purging?

Karmu: No they have various uses and effects. The bitter aloes and the goldenseal are used for purging some are used for cooling off the blood, or raising the energy level. We have a combination that takes your energy right up. Capsules of goldenseal and aloes combined with the manipulation of certain acupuncture points will make you want to fly.

Questioner: Do you take any herbs regularly?

Karmu: I take them regularly myself, yes. You never get sick, you never get tired and you feel good all the time.

Questioner: Same ones?

Karmu: Well we mix them up, it depends upon what's wrong with you. We use a basic herbal preparation but again it depends on wrong with you. If you blow your breath in your palm and you can't smell anything you're pretty clean inside.

Questioner: How did you learn all this?

Karmu: It has been in the family for generations and passed down. My father was an Ethiopian Jew; my mother was Chinese and black, and this and that. They were witch doctors so it came naturally.

Questioner: Do you offer classes for the use of herbs?

Karmu: Oh yes, we have classes. A woman was in a coma in a hospital in New York and I worked with one of my disciples who in turn went to New York and touched the woman and she came out of the coma.

Questioner: Just touched her!

Karmu: Well, she massaged her nerve centers—like acupuncture, only it's called acupressure.

Questioner: Not bad.

Karmu: No, I'd be glad to teach anyone who wants to learn.

Questioner: Could you give sort of a mini lesson?

Karmu: Right here?

Questioner: Sure.

Karmu: Step over, I'd be glad to. Okay, sit down here and turn your back towards me. We do a thing like this, we take the nerve centers and we activate them. When I get through you won't know it's you. Next time you take an examination come to me first and I'll make sure you pass it. How do you feel?

Questioner: I'm not sure what I went through.

Karmu: How do you feel anyway?

Questioner: Very light headed.

Karmu: Now your mind is very active, and you have a sense of wellness.

Questioner: It feels good. I should get that every morning.

Karmu: You see we have activated the nerve centers and we've giving the body balance. Stimulating the nerve centers this way creates what we call free mental association and balance. Everything works in unison like a finely coached ball-team.

KARMU'S MISSION

Ricardo: What is your mission in life?

Karmu: Our mission in life is to improve the lot of mankind. The mission involves handling problems that cross people's path and to improve them spiritually. Additionally, the mission is to improve mankind's health habits, and their way of life.

Ricardo: How is the church related to your healing work? I know you have answered this to some extent.

Karmu: The Church is a spiritual house where it is easier to bring out the God force in man for healing purposes.

Ricardo: Emanuel Swedenborg said there are three essentials of the Church: The divinity of Christ, the acknowledgment of the holiness of the word, and the life of charity, faith and love. What do you think of that Karmu?

Karmu: I think it is normal and natural. God is in all of us and if we have knowledge of him we can call God at any given time and get an answer. If you believe you are one with God, then that is the way it is.

Ricardo: Do you see your Church as being in the Christian tradition?

Karmu: The Church is in a spiritual tradition, which can be of any religion. Religion is something that man uses to call upon a higher being for help. A higher being within the self, which is God, it does not matter what religion or what type of religion; it all has the same purpose. The elevation of mankind through calling his inner spiritual essence is an activation of the sleeping God within.

Ricardo: If you were in my place as the interviewer, what question would ask about the Church of Karmu?

Karmu: The questions have been pretty well asked; you have acknowledged the purpose of the Church is to improve one's lot in life by calling upon the divinity, the spiritual higher being, to elevate one to a better place.

ON RACISM IN AMERICA

Ricardo: How do you see the condition of black people in America today?

Karmu: They are led around. They have what you call "token offerings". A few blacks are working the better jobs, and when they work there long enough they are cast out. They generally are going on what you call a backward run.

Ricardo: Is racism still widespread in America?

Karmu: Definitely, you have people who are told by their fathers and their mothers that people in other races are not like us. They are not the same as us. They are a different color and a different religion and they can't hope to compete with us. That's the general size of it.

Ricardo: Why does racism exist in this country?

Karmu: It exists because the blacks were brought here as slaves. The white man believed that blacks were inferior to him. The white man spoke, the black man jumped. He used black women for sex. The black man worked from dark to dark. A white man was considered in ill grace if he taught a black man to read and write. The fact that the blacks underwent these hardships made him strong. When you deprive a person he becomes stronger. Struggling makes him sharper. The best fighter is a hungry fighter. The black man is hungry, therefore, he is a better fighter, he is a survivor—they made him a survivor.

Ricardo: What do you think black people can do to improve their condition in America?

Karmu: They have to stick together, pick out the right politicians who have promise and have proven they can do something and put them in office; no nonsense, no foolishness. If they prove they can help, put them in. There are enough black people that if they vote in the same way they will effect change.

Ricardo: How has America benefited by the presence of black people?

Karmu: He aided the culture and strengthened their breed by mingling the blood. There are hidden blacks, whites with black ancestors, who have aided the white man's culture. Twenty-five percent of the inventions in this country were by blacks. Eight of your American presidents were hidden blacks. Many of your greatest heroes, like Matthew Henson, the black man who discovered the North Pole, were black. The best athletes are black; need I say more, black people contribute.

Ricardo: What do you see as the major problem facing this country?

Karmu: The major problem facing this country is how to give the country back to the people. It is ruled by politicians who have one thing in mind, their ego. The fact that they are white, the fact that they are the ruling class. The fact that they control the purse strings inflates their ego and they overlook other people. That's the reason why their airplanes don't fly and their ships sink in the ocean and they're being out-produced by the Japanese, Russians, Germans, and the Czechoslovakians. They'll be a third-rate country if they don't improve.

Ricardo: Will Blacks play a role in solving the problems?

Karmu: Definitely! There's no question about it. They're forging a way to the front. They're learning to take care of themselves. They want to take part in government. They want to know what's going on. This is our country too, and the problems are our problems. Let us learn about it so we can take the necessary steps to help solve the problems.

Ricardo: Will the United States maintain its prominence in the world today?

Karmu: I don't think so. The Germans and Japanese are out-producing them, out-maneuvering them, beating them by billions of dollars. The Japanese are exporting more than they are importing. Anytime a country gives you more than they take in, that demonstrates that they have the edge.

Ricardo: How did the United States lose its stronghold?

Karmu: By believing in white supremacy and by exploiting people. It's similar to the fall of the Roman Empire. Those in power become weak. They take to alcohol and orgies. The fall of the American Empire parallels the fall of the Roman and Greek Empire. The people become weak through success and stop working.

KARMU'S TRIP TO MEXICO

Ricardo: Karmu, where did you go in Mexico?

Karmu: A place called Cancun.

Ricardo: What kind of accommodations did you have?

Karmu: We stayed in a nice little house about 150 feet from the Ocean, which was accessible to tourist.

Ricardo: What kind of people did you encounter?

Karmu: We met a lot of tourist, but primarily we met Mayan Indians and Mexican people from all parts of Mexico. It's a new town and they are building it up. I met one man name Fernando who was building a 500 acre preserve for wildlife.

Ricardo: What similarities did you notice between Mexican people and American people?

Karmu: Mexican people are much kinder. They take you into their homes and exercise hospitality. They make you feel like one of them.

Ricardo: So, you like the Mexicans very much?

Karmu: The Mexican people set you on a pedestal, especially healers.

Ricardo: What kinds of ailments did you encounter while working with the people?

Karmu: Most of them had trouble with their teeth from drinking coke cola and improper diet. There are a lot of proteins they don't get enough of and they drink too much beer. They have the known ailments like diabetes, heart troubles, and stress related disorders. The big problems stem from improper diet, improper teeth care and stress.

Ricardo: What do their diet consist of?

Karmu: There diet consists of tortias, beans, mangoes, coconuts, greens; they eat tomatoes and lot of fruit and a lot of their diet revolves around beans.

Ricardo: Are the ailments you encountered there different from those Americans have?

Karmu: Yes, they don't have as much heart troubles. Most of the people lead a simple life. Things don't bother them too much.

Ricardo: How do they relax?

Karmu: They take time off during the day and sit in the sun or read the newspaper or sew.

Ricardo: And for a good time?

Karmu: Oh everybody knows each other and they gather together to play and dance.

Ricardo: It really sounds like you were well received there.

Karmu: Oh yeah, best time in my life.

Ricardo: So you would consider going back there? Living there?

Karmu: I'm considering going back but I don't know about living there. I think there may be a revolution there.

Ricardo: Are you talking about a change in government?

Karmu: Yes, the present government is corrupt and is creating too much friction.

Ricardo: So this is one of the things you learned while in Mexico?

Karmu: I learned that the air is clean, that the water is alright, that people get up early and work hard. Also, a lot of people live by fishing and that things are fairly inexpensive.

Ricardo: Did you experience any racism?

Karmu: None what-so-ever. In fact when someone asked me questions they were all in Spanish and they were amazed when I answered back in English.

Ricardo: Why do you think you didn't have to deal with racism?

Karmu: Because the Mexicans control their own destiny. They don't like the Americans. They don't like so-called gringos until gringos prove they can treat Mexicans fairly. In fact, they are suspicious of all gringos because they have been treated very badly by gringos in the past.

Ricardo: Is there any way in which Mexican culture is superior to American culture?

Karmu: Well is teaches you to take care of your family. Families are very close, and you respect the elder people; you learn to revere them for their advice, wisdom and knowledge.

Ricardo: Is there any way in which American culture is superior to Mexican culture? What do we have over them culturally?

Karmu: Well we use to have superior education, but I question if that's true now. They've got hundreds of Cuban teachers, directors, doctors, and so on, that are teaching the people to take care of themselves. They're doing a great job.

Ricardo: I think most Americans would look at that as communist influence.

Karmu: They call it a socialist government.

Ricardo: A more equitable form of government?

Karmu: That's right.

Ricardo: What did you learn about Mexico lore, myth, tradition, history and things like that?

Karmu: I would say their friendliness. They are very, very friendly. They take time out to talk with you and make you feel loved. Everyone isn't in a big hurry.

Ricardo: Did you meet any special individuals?

Karmu: The women next door would bring us fish. The man downstairs would bring us coconuts. The man with the fishing boat wanted to take me out on his boat. They made me feel loved and wanted—open doors and open hands. They kissed me on the cheek.

Ricardo: Why do you think it is that in general Americans know so little about Mexicans?

Karmu: One, because they're not taught. Two, because the media portrays Mexicans as illiterate people who have no common sense; backward people who take three-hour siestas and don't do anything.

Ricardo: Did you see yourself as having a special mission?

Karmu: I thought I could renew their way of healing. They had a name for me that means ancient healer. One who deals with roots and heals with faith and the laying-on-of-hands.

Ricardo: Curandero?

Karmu: That's the word.

Ricardo: Do you see yourself as having achieved that mission?

Karmu: Oh, definitely. There are Mexicans coming here to continue learning healing, especially some of the well-to-do ones, and if I go back there I'll be teaching.

Ricardo: Any other special insights that you gained?

Karmu: They don't worry too much about religion. The church has failed them as far as they are concerned and they have given up on religion.

Ricardo: That's very interesting. I tend to think of Mexicans as very religious, very Catholic as a matter of fact.

Karmu: They have given up on the Catholic religion. They didn't go to Church on Sunday where I was. They would go fishing.

Ricardo: Would you say that there is another religion developing among those people or are they letting that aspect go?

Karmu: They were brought up on religion and the religion betrayed them as far as I can see. It didn't do anything for them.

MARCH, 1984

Ricardo: Do you treat individuals for cancer often?

Karmu: Quite often

Ricardo: Can you give me some idea of the number of people that you have worked with?

Karmu: About 10,000.

Ricardo: That is a lot of people can you tell me about the treatments?

Karmu: You have to penetrate their subconscious and condition the mind. Let them know there is an unlimited higher power that will help them.

Ricardo: Are you saying you have been able to inspire?

Karmu: Well you also have to cleanse the body and free up the energy centers. Free up the mind, the brain, the back, the coccyx at the base of the spine, the legs and feet, the whole body. Then you have them take a herbal bath to further heal them. Then put them on the proper herbal products, and put them on a special diet. A cleansing diet featuring garlic, onions, spinach, and other similar healing foods. We can heal them in this way, sometimes in as few as two visits. I healed one cancer patient that the hospital sent home to die. We had him pray, had his wife pray for him, had his neighbors pray for him, we cleansed him, and put him on a nutritious diet. We hit all the bases. The man is well now.

Ricardo: Can you tell me about another successful case?

Karmu: There was a school teacher who had a mastectomy, and came to me very depressed and in terrible condition due to constant pain. I got her taking daily baths in a herbal cleansing solution and I got her to stop drinking alcohol and smoking. We purged her system, got her reading the Holy Bible and got her to exercise daily. She's happy now, she found relief.

Ricardo: What are some of the causes of cancer?

Karmu: Some of the contributing factors are stress, lack of money, uncertainty, job insecurity, toxic chemicals, and pollution in the air.

Ricardo: Are there certain people who are predisposed to developing cancer?

Karmu: Yes, people who are neurotic, and people who worry a lot, worriers. People who don't work enough with their hands, people who work with their hands tend to be more happy-go-lucky. These people tend not to get cancer. People with domestic problems and lots of stress run into these problems. People who have lots of time on their hands, people who worry a lot and don't exercise get cancer.

Ricardo: Are their certain lifestyles that lead to people becoming more vulnerable?

Karmu: Yes, people who don't take care of themselves and people with nerve raking jobs, like bank presidents, airline pilots, and professors with too much responsibility. Students who don't get enough rest, or those who see their life as a failure because they can't get a good job.

Ricardo. What can be done to prevent this illness?

Karmu: I would suggest seeing a therapist to help solve the problems, and make them feel better. Exercise, laughter, proper nutrition and prayer are all good ways to prevent this problem.

Ricardo: How about treating AIDS, have you treated AIDS?

Karmu: Once you become sexually active the body acquires a certain amount of disease. If the body gets weakened by such things as drug use and the body isn't cleansed, the germs in the body can cause the immune system to break down. Some people are what we call known carriers. Treating it is pretty much like treating cancer, condition the mind, cleanse the body, and give them exercises to do.

Ricardo: How about treating herpes?

Karmu: We haven't been able to cure it but we've been able to stop re-occurrences. Through medications and cleansing the system we can keep it in check. Stress can trigger it.

Ricardo: What's the best way to prevent it?

Karmu: Make sure your partner has been checked—good hygiene is important.

Ricardo: Can you say a little about diabetes?

Karmu: Diabetes is generally something you inherit, but in some cases eating too much sugar can play a part in causes it. Too much sugar and the wrong diet can throw the body out of balance. You treat it with insulin and proper nutrition, including such foods as onion, garlic, and grains.

Ricardo: What causes arthritis?

Karmu: Well you might inherit it or you could acquire it. People who work jobs where they experience a lot of contrast in weather are disposing themselves to it—like people who work under water.

Ricardo: How do you treat it?

Karmu: Here again the right exercise, the proper herbs and the right diet and a person can be fine.

Ricardo: Could you talk a little about another one of your famous cases?

Karmu: We have a case right now of a woman about 20 years old who would get so tired she could barely even walk up a flight of stairs. We worked on her charkas and freed up her whole system. Now she is working full time again and saving her money, her frame of mind has changed. If she keeps up with her exercise and eats the proper foods, I believe she will continue to be just fine.

Ricardo: It sounds like your treatment is pretty much always the same?

Karmu: The treatment depends on the individual, what ailment they have and how far the disease has advanced. For example, in advanced forms of cancer we might not be able to do anything about it. You have to remember most people have germs in their systems that can cause these various illnesses but it's kept under control as long as they stay healthy. When under a lot of stress those germs can become a problem.

Ricardo: That's probably enough right there, thanks Karmu.

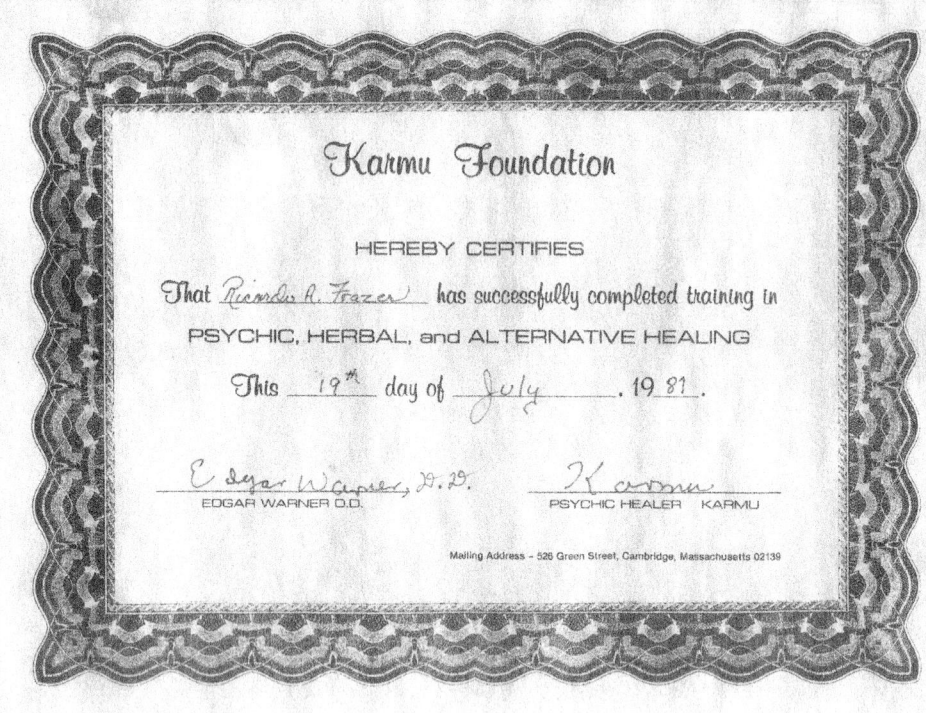

Chapter Ten

Channeling Session with Karmu and Frida Waterhouse On June 6, 1976

Frida: We're no longer on the John the Baptist trip where we're saving all souls; that sounds awfully tough don't it.

Karmu: Not necessarily.

Frida: All right but what we are on now is the Aquarian Age cusp, and what we're trying to do is use discrimination. What we place on the altar is not the sacrificial lamb; what we place on the altar is the sacrament done willingly, freely and lovingly; or the Divine ones will not accept it. It's the same thing God asked me last year, "Will you consent to stay on the Earth plane another fifteen to twenty years and I don't want it as a sacrificial lamb." I said, "Lord, I'll have to think that one over. First of all, I would have a contract with you that you are going to help heal this body because I can't stay here otherwise. I'm going to have to really know that this is, what I can do without sacrificing myself." So it took me two solid months until finally I went back and made this covenant, "I'll stay as long as you help me maintain this body and I'll do the work you want me to do." Then I found through the channeling of a very high person that it hadn't permeated every cell of my body and now what remains for me to do is to totally accept being here because there is a great longing for me to go where I really belong.

Karmu: Where do you belong?

Frida: Not here. Holy are thou, O Lord of the Universe. Holy are Thou who makes our heart mouth warm. Holy are Thou the vast and mighty ones, Lord of the Light and of the Darkness. For Thine is the Kingdom and the power and the glory forever. Amen.

I am hearing the music and the words of Hosannah on the Highest. Do you know where the music is I am speaking of? Hosannah on the Highest. Hosannah to the Lord.

It has been written in words of fire that the faithful of the Lord shall in true humility walk the paths that he has so carefully selected for them; for his purpose, for his honor, in joyful celebration.

There are those who are chosen and there are those who choose to be chosen and blessed are their names. It may ameliorate their circumstances and only serves to deplete your resources. The compassion of the Christ, whether it be the Buddha, the Krishna, Master Jesus, Lao Tzu, or whatever; is very impersonal and objectified; there is no personal subjective identification with a victim because it's not so much a victim of circumstances, as it is a victim of the effect of its own cause. When you can understand clearly and know beyond a shadow of a doubt that most people have placed themselves at some time or place, whether this life cycle or another, into those circumstances which are going to teach them the lessons that they need to learn and also to reclaim their karmic debts, then you will administer the healing energy's of the christian ones, the christian forces, and they are universal, not of one religion; with greater discrimination. Yes, you are your brother's keeper but it is not necessary to be like unto your brother subjectively on any level in order to help him, in fact it could hinder him, not always but it could do this. Therefore beloved, weep not because the children of the Earth are murderous, one towards another, pray instead and put them in the hands of God, and in the light, that they may be illuminated too, to see the truth of their relationships one to another, that they are truly brethren.

Basically you are related to the Earth Mother and Mother Nature but what you must do and where your strength must be attained if you will do the highest good for this life cycle, is to worship and recognize the divine mother. Mother nature exerts her control in many ways on the Earth plane and it is through her that many healings are done but there are many higher energies that can by-pass her and come from the divine Mother; a much more refined energy that can only be used for highly developed instruments can damage them, believe it or not. Therefore, before you touch anyone who is in a highly evolved state you must pray and ask very carefully whether you can bring through the energies that can match them. I have been badly damaged by healers that have helped me. I almost lost her life several times because of this. That's why we're mentioning this, this is not being said in criticism but we feel that there are higher octaves in the music within you of the most high to which you can attune and to which you can attain but it is not done on an instinctual process, it has to be done through prayer and meditation and gradually refining your instrument so that the cellular tissues and every cell in your body makes changes. Now in a refinement process we must warn you there will be times when you will not have as much strength because there will be cells literally dying that have to do with the old order, the old patterns, but if you wish, you can attain a higher refinement of evolution; of body, of spiritual body and of healing itself, the essence of healing. That's done less on the instinctual level and more from the level of the highest guidance, and that has to be done with very delicate attunement at all times, that is a promise and a prediction, but the choice is always yours. On an emotional level, however, the time may come, not may come, but will come, when the curtain will come down on your present environment and you will be finished here but that's not in the immediate future, now that's a prediction.

You are most fortunate in that you have a great deal of protection, and that's why you can work with people who have possessions, but you need everything that God taught you today, and before you leave he will give you more protection. You must be sure always to ask that your body be completely cleansed and neutralized, you should do that regularly. Another thing is, if you are working with anyone who is in a great deal of pain or who has a condition that is contagious or a great deal of fear or a great deal of negativity; place a lock in your elbow so nothing can come past this, put a protection on your solar plexus because that's where you absorb a lot of it, in fact place a sword and a shield on your whole heart. Guard your solar plexus energy so none of the negative energies can enter and you can do it in light, I'll tell you about it later when we finish.

Basically, you are a healing instrument and one of the things you have done partially and in the future can do more of, is the alignments of the chakras, so that an instrument can receive more clearly without interference due to imbalances of the body.

Everything we do in the way of healing, of course, not only affects a physical body but it reflects on the emotional body, the mental body, and the etheric body called the spiritual body. There will come a time beloved when you will heal bodies not so much by touch but by your presence and by the auric field you exude and by the love and divine grace that will come through you; you will be that instrument.

Was anything said that you don't understand?

Karmu: No, I understand

Frida: We find no arrogance in this instrument, simply a surcharge of
    over-concern about his fellow man, on an emotional subjective level

which is not helpful for him or his work, and if he asks to be cleansed and purified and neutralized, if he remembers to ask for protection morning, noon, and night and at all times when he's in any kind of danger or in the path of any negativity, he will speedily attain the highest realms. To obtain protection he should cocoon himself in the white light of the Christ, or the gold light of the Godhead, or a color that seems most healing to him. He can imagine this color and see himself painting it; whatever it takes to do this, this cocooning. Ask for protection first thing in the morning and the last thing at night. If he has a symbol whether it be a cross, an ankh, whatever symbol that has meaning for him; he should cover himself with this symbol in light regularly, morning, noon and night and at times of stress. Go Thou then with great blessing, so be it Lord and so it is. Amen.

INTERVIEW WITH ONE OF KARMU'S CLIENTS

Ricardo: So is the ailments you came to Karmu for cleared up?

Client: Sort of stable. Karmu has increased the healing process tremendously. Absolutely tremendously and I'm now what you call basically healthy. I just get these spasms every now and then because I over-work. I work too much and karmu calls me on it.

Karmu: We have an exchange and we also exchange energy. I can hold her in my arms and in 20 minutes she's like new.

Client: Oh yeah! I can feel it, he is now working on a rash, a demon, that I've got, that was due to emotional strain, it was due to physiological things, it was due to extreme stress, due to over-work, and just some foolish things I knew better about and didn't listen to, and on one hand he removed a blockage here in my chest, it was really intense, I was having chest pains, and he opened it up, and my whole left arm got real painful. It was real intense and I passed out, but it opened it up and since then I've made tremendous progress. A week ago my face was, what color was my face Karmu?

Karmu: Red

Client: Well it was more than red, it was scarlet and black and so puffy at times that I couldn't really see through my eyes and now it's like I have new skin.

Ricardo: How often do you come here?

Client: As often as I can, I come about once a week.

Karmu: She heals me you know. We have a thing between us that means we have to stay together for another 30 or 40 years at least.

Client: That's because he can't get rid of me.

Karmu: It's because whatever I need I can get from her. If I need encouragement I can get it. She's always there and I've come to depend on her. She's a part of my life.

Ricardo: You're referring to that exchange that goes on between you two.

Karmu: There's a spiritual and physical exchange. I boost her up to the world and she can feel it. She goes higher and she is going to rebuild the state of Wyoming for us.

Client: He's my natural high. Ha! Ha! Ha! Ha!

INTERVIEW WITH SANDRA FRAZER

Ricardo: How were you introduced to Karmu?

Sandra: You introduced me to him in October of 1983. I wanted to do some healing work around gaining confidence.

Ricardo: Was he a healer, in your mind?

Sandra: Yes, that's why I wanted to do some work with him

Ricardo: Why do you think he attracted so many patients?

Sandra: There are a lot of people looking for alternative help

Ricardo: What do you see as the source of his ability to help people?

Sandra: I believe he had healing powers, and his own perception of how to help others.

Ricardo: Is this an ability anyone can have or was he special?

Sandra: I would say he was unique. I don't know if everyone has this ability. From my experience with him, I saw him study people. He helped people understand their own potential. Karmu was acutely aware of himself and his ability.

Ricardo: Did he have a gift or was it his ability developed?

Sandra: I think it was developed.

Ricardo: What's your most vivid memory of Karmu?

Sandra: I remember the work he did on me. He once had me try to do some healing work on him. I remember believing in him and in his capability. I don't think he was ordinary. He was extraordinary. I think he really wanted to help people and see them well. He was concerned about his fellow man.

Ricardo: Do you remember any of his sayings?

Sandra: He called people a triple movie star. He was real bright that way. Always lifting people's spirit. He always tried to encourage people.

Ricardo: Do you feel he influenced you in any way?

Sandra: I guess my beliefs. I remember there were people who lived in his house or stopped through who could be negative about what he was doing. I felt their negativity brought people down and didn't help. I think if more people were like Karmu the world would be a better place. I was looking at the volume of people like Karmu in the world and I haven't seen a lot like him. It's sad because it's all about money now.

INTERVIEW WITH A CAMBRIDGE WOMAN WHO KNEW KARMU

How were you introduced to Karmu?
 I met Karmu because my housemate Janice was going to him for healings and blue medicine. Many of my housemates eventually went to him and it became a place where I would see Karmu, hang out with him, and other people from the neighborhood.

Why do you think he attracted so many patients?

I think Karmu's warmth, humor, accessibility, generosity drew people to him. People tended to feel better just being with him because he was such a force of nature, funny, loving, and confident in his healing abilities.

Did Karmu have special healing abilities or was his ability commonplace?

I heard lots of stories about Karmu healing people of cancer, when western medicine had failed them. I could never bring myself to drink blue medicine, but I bathed in it quite a lot and I felt better after seeing Karmu. I never saw him for anything life threatening, but things like the flue, a bad cough, stuff like that.

Was he the "real thing?"

I think he was the real thing, and fell into the category of a faith healer. He healed with his energy, which was lively and caring, earthy and full of humor. Getting people to laugh and open up especially when they weren't feeling well was a big part of his appeal. He knew how to ease people's suffering, to set them at ease, to help them open up and talk about what was bothering them, he had a roaring laugh and a big barrel chest and belly, strong arms, kind of like a Sumo wrestler, but not at all intimidating.

What made him a great human being or an ordinary person?

He was an ordinary man, living very simply, with an unusual amount of vim.

What is your most vivid memory of Karmu?

I was feeling suddenly really crumby so I went to see Karmu. I had seen him at least six times in the past and he had never said to me what he said this particular time. He checked me out, asked me a bunch of questions, and suddenly he pinned me with his eyes and asked me pointedly, when no one else was in the room, if I had recently performed oral sex on a man. I said yes. He asked me if it was the first time I'd been with him. I said yes. He asked me if I'd swallowed any of his semen and I said yes. He told me this man was troubled and I had taken on his negative energy when I swallowed his semen and that I was not to do this again unless I was very very sure a man's energy was pure. This was in the 70's before AIDs and the man I'd been intimate with had been celibate and a yogi for quite a while when I met him. I forget what remedy Karmu gave me or told me to take, but it left a lasting impression on me.

Do you recall any of Karmu's sayings?

I remember every time I saw Karmu near the end of a session he would laugh, thump himself on the chest and thunder: How can we lose with the system we use!

Karmu seemed to be many things to many people. How do you regard Karmu? Teacher? Healer ? Guru? etc. Please explain.

Definitely not a guru. I've had a guru and Karmu was not this to me. Not a teacher either, although I suspect he was to you because you lived in his home and were a lot closer to him than I was. I'd say he was a faith healer.

BIOGRAPHICAL STATEMENT

I'm 57 yrs old, have lived in Cambridge since the late 70's, in the part of town now known as Riverside, where Karmu lived. I am a singer songwriter, supporting myself as a chef, a garden and flower designer, and realtor over the years while continuing to compose and sing. I got into organic gardening, whole foods, and holistic healing in my early 20's. Although I believe in having a good primary care physician keeping tabs on my health, I tend to maintain my health through nutrition, exercise, meditation, singing, herbs, homeopathy and acupuncture. Most people think I'm 10-15 years younger than I am and I attribute this to genes, lifestyle and a positive attitude. I have always reached out to healers when out of balance or ill. In general I'm healthy but I've been gravely ill and injured a few times. Finding the right people to help me heal and being willing to face my inner demons and emotional challenges with honesty, courage and compassion has made all the difference in my healing process and soul's journey. I write songs about what I encounter along the way and although personal, they are universal. My 14 year old son has been raised on organic whole foods, close to nature and music since he was a baby. He gets homeopathic remedies, herbs and acupuncture treatments on the rare occasions when he is ill. Twice in his life he's taken antibiotics. I've consulted a medical intuitive who's a friend of the family, when my son or I have had something chronic or difficult to diagnose. I feel blessed that Nina is there for us when we need her. I also feel blessed to have an amazing primary care doctor who is a healer, teacher and jazz pianist. I am part of a long time Vipassana meditation class in Cambridge, taught by an old friend who is an inspiring teacher. This path, deepened by the teachings of people like Pema Chodron, plays an important part in my worldview and approach to my own being. As one of my songs says:

> It's all about connection,
> the simple joy to be
> standing in your shoes
> with authenticity

HEALING WORK

Dear Karmu,

I am the young woman—the writer—who went to the hospital for a bone marrow transplant, last November. I came to you, one of the skeptics, and I come to you again, with thanks. Often, I think of you and as you might expect, I can't stop the smile that comes with the thought. I try to tell people about you but I find "telling is insufficient." I risk the danger of sounding trite, and everyone has the usual reaction: "Faith healer? You must have been desperate . . . etc. . . . ." I was desperate, but to me, that doesn't matter. We come to our deepest realizations in moments of desperation.

I have been a wonderful success at the hospital—a walking miracle. I have had *no* complication. And now, I am working at the hospital doing research on the disease I had. I talk with patients who have what I *had* and I encourage them to believe in their will, in positive thinking, and in healing-type imagery. I have to be a little discreet about it because there is a lot of resistance to these "weird, hippy-like methods."

I admire you; respect you, because you always encourage me to follow my heart, to do what I felt was best. I chose the hospital route because it was what I was brought up with; but knowing I had seen you, *felt* you, made a huge difference in life. I will be by to see you within the next month. I was reading some of your "propaganda" tonight and couldn't resist writing.

Affectionately,
Jessica

Chapter Eleven

Psychological Wellness

TRANSPERSONAL PSYCHOLOGY

Rituals can play an important part in human wellness. One area of western psychology that investigates the phenomenon of ritual is transpersonal psychology. Transpersonal psychology investigates phenomena that are beyond the personal, such as trance. Trance can be induced through various means such as meditation, dance, religious ceremony, drumming, hypnosis, and so on. When practiced as rituals, these activities can bring us into higher levels of consciousness. Artists, poets, musicians, and other creative individuals often utilize this ability. They themselves may not understand the process and simple apply their craft—thus creating from inner sources.

Repetitive behavior can be viewed as having ritualistic qualities, however, more traditional rituals tends to embody deeper symbolic meaning. For example, in a frequently preformed Christian ritual, we "eat of the body and drink of the blood of Christ," as a way of remembering Jesus. The ritual brings us into the spirit of Christ, and the symbols (bread and wine) represent that which is no longer physically present. The symbol is not the thing, but symbols can communicate when words fail us. Through the ritual we experience the divine.

Rituals can move individuals to heightened states of awareness. A kind of grounding or connecting with one's creative impulse, or source. Rituals may even transform our lives by altering the way we perceive, in profound ways. Revelations and illumination may occur during ritually-induced states that change our reality.

All art forms can involve ritual. Poetic insight may light the way. Musicians are often transported to higher spheres. Dancers may never come down from a leap of faith. The painter's brush may move the hand. The arts can foster divine inspiration, which seem to come from everywhere, and no-where in particular. Healing can occur through ritual.

Transpersonal psychotherapy can assist an individual in realizing his or her spiritual nature and potentials. Transpersonal therapists and holistic healers can help the client better understand his or her spiritual work or spiritual journey. The therapist may aid the client in formulating or conceptualizing their relationship with the divine. Many people struggle with the concept of spirituality and are confused about how spirituality relates to them. Religious beliefs are often highly personal and unique to the particular individual. Transpersonal therapists and holistic healers assist their patients in building a personal relationship with, and strengthening communication with their divinity.

ALTERNATIVE HEALING

Deepak Chopra

Deepak Chopra is a contemporary medical doctor whose approach to medicine and health care incorporates eastern philosophy and religion, along with his western scientific training. He writes and lectures extensively and has had dynamic results, which has attracted tremendous interest and enthusiasm among readers, listeners, and patients.

Chopra believes that success in life includes good health, energy, enthusiasm for life, fulfilling relationships, creative freedom, emotional and psychological stability, a sense of well-being, and peace of mind (Chopra, 1994). All of these things are possible if we nurture and develop our divinity (Chopra, 1994). Seven of Deepak Chopra's identified principles provide a roadmap for navigating our life journey toward these goals. According to Chopra:

1. Our spirit is a field of awareness that connects everything to everything instantly.
2. Our inner dialogue reflects our inner power.
   a. I am independent of the good or the bad in people
   b. I am neither superior nor inferior to other people
   c. I have no desire to have power over, manipulation of or control other people.
3. Our intentions have infinite organizing power.
4. I know how to rise above emotional turbulence through sobriety and witnessing.
5. Nurturing love and relationships is the most important activity of my soul.

6. I embrace the masculine and feminine in my own being.
7. I am aware of the conspiracy of improbabilities. There is no such thing as coincidence.

ANALYTICAL PSYCHOLOGY

Jung's Seminal Contribution

Carl Gustav Jung (1875-1961) was a Swiss born psychiatrist who worked to integrate his scientific education and professional training with his study of philosophy and religion. One result is a school of analytical psychology that uses the arts as vehicles for understanding individuals and helping them heal. Jung used art forms such as autobiographical writing, drawing, painting, poetry, and storytelling, to help the individual gain greater understanding of self, and move towards wholeness. Jung rejected the striving for perfection and replaced it with the striving for wholeness. Achieving wholeness involves the development of our potentials, integrating our shadow into our persona, and addressing our complexes. It also involves developing our masculine side if we are females, our feminine side if we are males, and balancing these masculine/feminine qualities.

Jung felt that the purpose of life was to give it meaning. Meaning is generally found in doing the necessary psychological and spiritual work—as humans, we develop issues which need recognition and resolution. We cannot grow psychologically unless we grow spiritually, and we cannot attain our spiritual maturity unless we mature psychologically.

By becoming who and what we most uniquely are, we accomplish our great work. In perfection one identifies with an ideal and attempts to realize that ideal. In wholeness one incorporates ideals as goals but strives to realize one's full potential. Self-realization is a central concept in Jung's analytical psychology. Jung also developed the concept of synchronicity—the perception of meaningful coincidences. Jung believed that we live in a unified reality where everything is meaningful and nothing is meaningless. Each moment and event has its own deep reality. We live in a universe were coincidence is non-trivial.

Jung's insights were geared towards helping individuals lead better and healthier lives. Jung incorporated Asian and African philosophy and religious studies into his scientific framework. The result is a mystical psychology that incorporates spiritual and psychological insights and approaches into treatment.

HUMANISTIC PSYCHOLOGY

Maslow's Self-Actualization

Humanistic psychology adopted Jung's striving towards wholeness as a central motivation in the development of personality. Psychologists such as Abraham Maslow, Carl Rodgers, Kurt Goldstein, and others referred to this motivation as "self-actualization". An actualizing person is someone who has identified her/his uniqueness and is expressing that uniqueness. Self-actualization is conceptualized as both a goal and a process. Once activated, self-actualization is an on-going process of becoming—stages or plateaus from which to operate, function, or simply be.

Abraham Maslow (1908-1970) believed that the major goal in life was to actualize our inherent potentials. He thought that individuals moved towards actualization sequentially by meeting and addressing a hierarchy of needs. Humans have two sets of needs—basic needs and growth needs. In order to move towards self-actualization (a growth need), individuals must first address their basic needs. Maslow thought that once the basic needs were gratified, growth needs, including the need for self-actualization become salient.

Once physiological needs are adequately met, safety needs become salient. Once safety needs are met, individuals move on to love and belonging. If these needs are satisfied, concerns shift to esteem needs. The highest stage is that of self-actualization—the striving to become the best that we can be. Individuals also seek to know and understand.

Maslow's theory of personality development generated great interest among humanistically-oriented individuals. However, Maslow's attempt to empirically validate the concept of self-actualization proved difficult. Subsequent attempts have not fared better (Ryckman, 2000). The difficulty confronted by these efforts suggests that Maslow's concept of self-actualization was too loosely defined.

When Maslow died, he had begun the work to develop the concept of self-actualization into a more functional construction. Maslow worked to develop a transpersonal psychology aimed at integrating self-transcendence into western psychology. This was a much needed addition, since self-actualization in the context of western society became too self-centered.

To truly self-actualize one must transcend the self, serve others, and flow. To flow means to be totally absorbed in the ever present moment. Flowing requires a great deal of skill obtained through disciplined work and the matching of one's ideals with challenging goals.

INDIVIDUAL PSYCHOLOGY

Adler's Social Interest

Alfred Adler (1929a) regarded social interest as a human potential that must be developed. He theorized that the development of social interest was motivated by efforts to overcome feelings of inferiority. Adler thought that all individuals experience feelings of inferiority, resulting from the long period of dependency on others during infancy and childhood. Social interest was thought to develop from the successful resolution of the feelings of inferiority. Adler hypothesized that failure to fully resolve these feelings would result in a mistaken style of life. Examples of mistaken styles of life would include criminal behavior, neurosis, psychosis, alcoholism (Sulliman, 1973). Individuals can get involved in a myriad of mistaken styles, however, the most effective strategy for resolving the inevitable feelings of inferiority requires the development of social interest.

Deepak Chopra and Carl Jung developed procedures and approaches based in an incorporation of eastern philosophical and western scientific schools of thought regarding physical health and human wellness. Both thinkers, like Alfred Adler, implicated social interest as central in psychological health and wellness. Chopra contends that success is achieved by asking oneself and answering two key questions—how can I help? And how can I be of service?

Chopra says:

> "Everyone has a purpose in life . . . a unique gift or special talent to give to others. And when we blend this unique talent with service to others, we experience the ecstasy and exaltation of our spirit, which is the ultimate goal of all goals" (Chopra, 1994, p.93).

Chopra believes that when we connect our purpose to serving humanity by asking and answering these key questions, abundance and wellness unfold. When we express our unique talents in service to humanity we express our divinity. It is in this state of being that we self-actualize.

EASTERN PHILOSOPHY AND RELIGION

Archeological, paleontological, and anthropological evidence demonstrates that modern humans originated on the African continent and the first great civilizations were organized by these African people. The fertile equatorial lands surrounding the Nile River were most conducive for settlement and development of agrarian-based societies. Among the many contributions of African people was religion and philosophy. These two disciplines were considered to be one system with religion at the center. Religion was placed at the center of all life. Psychology was an integral and inseparable part of religion and philosophy.

Philosophy was a practical system for organizing knowledge. For example, the individual is related to the universe, as microcosm is related to macrocosm. In other words, everything in the universe was considered to be in the individual and everything in the individual was considered to be in the universe. The difference was simply a matter of scale—the individual was small while the universe was big. Everything was considered to be one whole with many different levels. To fully understand the universe, one had to understand how things functioned on Earth (as Above, so Below). To truly understand the individual, one had to understand the cycles embedded in cycles. Planets are part of the cycling universal order—thus the advent of Astrology, in Africa. Human activities such as planting, birthing, harvesting, and so on, were all harmonized with the rhythms and cycles of the sun and moon.

To the ancient Africans, the part was viewed as reflective of the whole, and the whole was viewed as reflected in the part. The laws of nature were viewed as based in evident irrationalities, and analysis meant identification of patterns inherent in phenomena. African philosophy emphasized the ever present moment and the indivisible unity of reality.

One implication of this African philosophy for western psychology is that subject and object are inseparable. Aristotle, Socrates, and Plato were well aware of Egyptian philosophy and incorporated it freely. Greek scholars re-interpreted the African worldview. Greek philosophers made rationality the basis of human thinking. This laid the foundation for splitting concepts such as mind-body, spirit-matter, self-other, subject-object, and so on. These philosophers laid the basis for the nineteenth century experimental psychology of Wilhelm Wundt, E.H. Weber, Gustav Fechner, and Hermann von Helmholtz. Kant also argued that it was impossible to apply rational analysis to the soul. Kant said "to know the nature of the soul was beyond the ability of human reason." He concluded that psychology could only be an empirical science. Kant's arguments provided the philosophy upon which Jakob Friedrich Fries, Johann Friedrich Herbart, and Friedrich Eduard Beneke developed the conceptualization of scientific psychology (Leary, 1978). Wilhelm Wundt is credited as the founder of modern scientific psychology. He accepted the Greek interpretation of psyche as mind, and attempted to determine the "elements of mind" through scientific investigation in the laboratory.

A purely rational empirical psychology is out of balance and leaves a major void. The ancient Africans developed the concept of psyche. Psyche was the soul, the Egyptian Sakhu, composed of levels within levels. Maslow recognized the need for western psychology to integrate the soul into its dominant paradigm, and develop a transpersonal psychology. The most comprehensive foundation for a transpersonal psychology is the paradigm developed by ancient Africans.

We must return to the ancient way of thinking of our-self as one with all things. The separation of mind and body, self and other, subject and object, is a useful heuristic, but when taken to the extremes we have taken it, it removes us from reality. All things are part of one whole. When we harm another human being, or harm the Earth with chemical pollutants, or force wildlife into extinction, we in fact harm ourselves because of the inextricable bond between all life.

ENERGETIC PSYCHOLOGY

Humans are electromagnetic beings that radiate and transmit energy. Electrical energy surges through our nervous system, our meridians and our entire being. Quantum theory can assist in the understanding of this energy. Energy is thought of as wave and particle. Particles are matter, waves are energy. When unobserved, sub-atomic particles behave as waves of possibility. When observed, the waves collapse into particles. Energy can be thought of simply as matter in motion. Albert Einstein, provided a mathematical formulation for the relationship between energy and matter ($E = MC^2$). Energy and matter are interchangeable since one form can be converted into the other.

The human body has a frequency at which it vibrates. Organs, glands, cells, and all components of the human body have vibratory frequency. Frequencies are composed of a key tone and its mathematical overtones, often referred to as a harmonic series. All things have frequencies that produce vibration, overtones, discord, and harmony.

The relatively slow rate at which the atoms of the body are moving and the relative density of this matter is partially responsible for the perception of human beings as more solid than space. However, the human being is composed of more space than matter. We are spirit energy at the most fundamental level. We have been conditioned to view humans as matter rather than energy. The various energy states or forms (e.g. light, heat, sound, etc.) are all part of one continuum that interacts with human energy. Humans are influenced by energy in the environment via receptor cells. These receptor cells perform the function of transducing or converting energy from the environment into a form of energy that our brain can work with—neurological energy or neurological impulses. Neurological impulses are transmitted via the peripheral nervous system to the spinal cord and brain for interpretation and action. This is one model of how the process works.

We can also become aware of things in ways that occur outside of these normal channels, since everything in the universe is interconnected, energetically. We can know directly without indirect mediation via transmission to the brain. Energy in the environment can interact directly with an individuals' energy field (a person's energy field has been referred to as an aura). The ability to perceive directly is sometimes referred to as intuition, psi, or other forms of psychic ability. This ability tends not to be highly developed in most individuals, however, many of us conceive of a future in which the use of this ability will be as commonplace as our thinking, hearing, feeling, tasting, smelling, and other similar human capacities.

Meditation has also been used for centuries to achieve higher consciousness, to connect with spiritual guides, and to strengthen contact with the sources of life. Meditation was probably used to discover the internal system of energy flow through the body known as the system of chakras and meridians. The meridians are channels in which energy flows throughout the body. Acupuncture, acupressure, massage, and other similar treatment modalities devised in the East are based on the meridians and chakras. The chakras are the centers of the energy system. When blockage occurs in these energy centers or channels of energy flow, illness of the body, mind, and soul can occur. Obstruction or blockage in any of the bodily systems can cause illness. Especially if the immune system, our bodies self-defense system, is not functioning optimally. Eastern forms of medicine often involve ways of unblocking or freeing up our blocked or trapped energy. Massage and acupressure involves direct manipulation of energy. Whereas with acupuncture, needles mediate the energy.

The ancient Egyptians were among the first to manipulate human energy in these ways. Energy manipulation was also much more elaborate. Pyramids operated essentially as a large lens that focused a specific frequency of infrared energy into specific sites in the pyramid (Amen, 1999). The vibratory frequency generated by the pyramidal structure liberated oxygen from carbon dioxide molecules and created an oxygen-ionized environment that promoted healing. Oxygen-enriched air enters the body though the breath and flows from the lungs to the kidneys, liver, heart, spleen and back into the lungs. Some of the breath provides energy for the function of the organs, and some is used in disease resistance. This energy, also known as chi, flows through a system of bodily channels or meridians. The power centers of this system are the charkas. Specific points along this system of meridians, can be manipulated with magnets, needles, pressure, laser and other mediums to effect the circulation of energy and cancel out disease. This approach to medicine was founded in ancient Egypt. One architect of early pyramids, Imhotep, was also a surgeon. It is possible that he conducted surgery in the ionized atmosphere generated in pyramids. While this is speculation, many pyramid secrets have yet to be revealed.

The ancient Egyptians placed the original source of all energy in the cosmos. Pyramids were placed in alignment with certain stars in the sky to maximize access to cosmic energy. For example, the Queen's chamber of Khufu's

Great Pyramid at Giza, points to the star Sirius in the constellation Canis Major. Sirius was a star of great importance to ancient Africans. The king's chamber of Khufu's pyramid points to Alnitak, a star in the belt of the constellation Orion. The constellation Orion was also of great significance to these Africans. Alignment with stars was part of a sacred geometry that laid a foundation for architectural structures that could transform and transmit energy.

EXERCISES

EXERCISES TO ACTIVATE THE IMAGINATION FOR PERSONAL GROWTH

The following exercises, based in the work of Carl Jung and Deepak Chopra, may be a useful way to increase self-knowledge, personal adjustment and personal growth. Active imagination can also open the way to reconciliation. Actively keeping an imaginative journal is a good way to explore ones unconscious or shadow. In this way we can be instruments for an inner and outer flow of events in accordance with the divine plan for our lives. The following are suggested questions (others can be added to the list). Write down your answers.

1. List three of your strongest fears
2. List three global fears (e.g. fears you have for the world)
3. List three things that really get under your skin or bug you about other people
4. I must admit, I am weak when it comes to _____
5. I really get angry with my parents (or child) when . . .
6. In the form of a poem, express your feelings about (a) fatherhood, (b) motherhood or (c) childhood
7. How can I be of service to others?
8. How can I help others?
9. List eight to twelve events that were milestones in your life
10. List every major spiritual experience you can remember
11. Hold a dialogue with an event or dream image from your past
12. Write a letter to a deceased person
13. Write a letter to a person you are in conflict with

We can use these exercises to identify and change unhealthy thoughts. Reality is a manifestation of thought. To get healthy, one must change unhealthy thought-forms into thoughts that foster wellness, joy, happiness, harmony and life. Unhealthy thoughts can summon chronic illnesses and dis-ease. Being is a process, and reality is a social construction.

Références

Amen, Nur Ankh (1999). The Ankh: African origins of electromagnetism. New York: A & B Publishers Group.

Amen, Ra Un Nefer (1990). Metu Neter: The Great Oracle of Tehuti and the Egyptian System of Spiritual Cultivation. Vol.1. NY: Khamit Corp.

Capra, F. (1991). The Tao of Physics: An exploration of the Parallels between Modern Physics and Eastern Mysticism. Boston: Shambhala.

Chopra, D. (1994). The Seven Spiritual Laws of Success: A Practical Guide to the Fulfillment of Your Dreams. California: A ber-Allen Publishing.

Leary, D.E. (1978). The Philosophical Development of the Conception of Psychology in Germany, 1780-1850. Journal of the History of the Behavioral Sciences, 14, 113-121.

Morton, T. Kelsey (1988). Christo-Psychology. New York: Crossroads Publishing Company.

Pike, G. (1980). The power of ch'i: The secrets of Oriental breathing for health and longevity.

Rama, S., Ballentine, R., Hymes, A. (1979). Science of Breath: A practical Guide. Pennsylvania: The Himalayan International Institute.

Ryckman, R. (2000). Theories of Personality. Connecticut: Wadsworth/ Thomson Learning. New York: Bell Publishing Company.

Chapter Twelve

The Crisis in American Health Care

The treatment of any medical condition requires treating the whole person, rather than simply treating the disorder. Few treatments are ever effective without the effort of the patient, yet often the psychology and the soul of the patient receives inadequate attention. In the effort to destroy a disease causing pathogen, the crucial role that the patient plays in the treatment is sometimes lost. The place of medical doctors and pharmacists in modern medicine is firmly established, the American medical system would collapse without them, but standard medicine cannot do it all. The American medical system needs help, and help is available in alternative and complement medicine. However, these systems are often ignored in the raging debate regarding how to best help the ailing American people and the ailing American health care system. Many therapies that are invaluable complements to standard medicine are not funded by insurance companies and the psychology of the individual patient is not enhanced during the treatment.

A vital component of any treatment protocol is the psychology of the person. The word psychology is made up of two words "psyche" and "ology." Ology is a Greek term that means "the study of." Psyche, is Greek translation of the African word "sakhu" which means soul. The ancients recognized people as souls in need of illumination. Any form of health care treatment must connect with and illuminate the patients' soul. For the body to heal the psyche must be engaged. Modern scientific psychology frequently measures this phenomenon and identifies it as the "placebo effect." Drug researchers know that when any drug is tested, approximately 20 to 30 percent of the people not receiving any active drug agent, those in the control group, may have a placebo effect.

In other words, they will respond as if they actually received the drugs being tested in the study.

While the placebo effect can be a nuisance for drug researchers, it is an aid in treatment, and it empirically validates the role of the mind in medical treatment. All health practitioners are not only treating a body, they are treating a mind, and a soul. In the effort to eradicated disease, practitioners using the standard medical model frequently lose sight of the vital role of the mind in treatment. Yet, it's not uncommon to hear a cancer patient say that they find their oncologist to be negative and depressing. All medical practitioners must inspire faith, hope, and belief in the recovery of their patients because these psychological components are critical dynamics in the treatment of any medical illness. Health care practitioners who mislead patients for financial gain are simply crooks. Practitioners who inspire hope, because of its life enhancing benefits, are doing their work.

Many areas of empirical research demonstrate effects of psychology on the body. Joy, laughter, love, happiness, and finding meaning in life, all effect changes in the body. The exact mechanism through which these effects occur has not yet been fully determined. The neuroendocrine and the immune systems appear to play a major role. The endocrine system is made up of glands that regulate a wide range of biological processes. The study of hormones, neurotransmitters, and peptides are widening the doors of our understanding. Psychoneuroimmunology (PIN) is a relatively new medical discipline that investigates the connection between the mind/brain, neuroendocrine and the immune systems. Studies in PIN demonstrate that what happens in the brain/mind has effects on the physiological and the immune systems. PIN research suggests that high levels of persistent anxiety can compromise the immune system. Anecdotal evidence also suggests that a terminally ill patient who is told that they have a certain amount of time to live, might die around the suggested time.

The focus of chiropractic therapy is transformation and greater expression. This is the vitalistic non-mechanistic approach to chiropractic health care. Among other factors, health is the product of a clear nervous system. One goal of chiropractic treatment is to unite the physical with the spiritual. Clearing spinal issues allows the body's innate intelligent life force to more fully express itself—increased health is the consequence.

Medical researchers have also identified the brain within our gut—the enteric nervous system, more commonly known as the second brain. Gut and psychology syndrome (gaps) research is beginning to demonstrate that the number and mix of toxins in the digestive system may cause different neurological and psychiatric symptoms. The identification of the precise biological mechanism linking the brain, the nervous system, and immune systems appears to be at hand.

The Immune Recovery Foundation (IRF) provides a host of alternative treatments to restore the immune system. These services are provided through a network of three Immune Recovery Clinics. IRF also collects and summarizes significant data with respect to the safe use of various allopathic and complementary treatment modalities. While some treatment protocols offered are not FDA approved, they can be requested by patients and given in the state of Georgia because of the provisions of the Georgia Access to Medical Practice Act.

The main focus of the Immune Recovery Clinics has been the use of complementary medical treatment with cancer patients who have refused or failed regular allopathic medical treatment for cancer. The clinic also specializes in the treatment of patients other health challenges including autoimmune disease, metabolic disease, celiac disease, multiple sclerosis, chronic fatigue, fibromyalgia, viral conditions, thyroid dysfunction, and many other conditions. The philosophy of the clinics is that a common concern in all health challenges is a suppressed immune system.

Cancer itself is able to suppress the immune system and does so as a protective mechanism. The immune system is programmed to destroy tumor cells. However, the immune suppression is in large part due to other pre-cancer conditions. Immune suppression allows the cancer to develop and survive. Cancer therapy must take immune suppression into consideration and restore immune function, if the cancer is to be adequately treated. Both alternative cancer therapy and especially integrative cancer therapy make immune restoration the keystone of their cancer treatment protocols. Treatment modalities offered at the Immune Recovery Clinics include Infusion therapies, IPT, Chemotherapies, Lymphatic Drainage, Hyperbaric therapy, Massage, Acupuncture, and much more.

The American health care system is in crisis. While over 17 percent of America's gross national product is spent on health care, the results are mediocre, when compared to other developed countries. The various health care systems in this country, including standard and complementary medicine, are not working well together. This is a critical juncture in American health care with many vital factors currently in the balance. While it is uncertain whether Americans are facing a revolution or an evolution in our health-care system, one thing is certain, the current structure is not currently working for the benefit of all people. Our current health-care system better serves those who are well financed. Change is required—perhaps a more vitalistic approach would serve us all much better.

Chapter Thirteen

Issues Relating Complementary and Non-Allopathic Health Care in America

The Immune Recovery Foundation was started in December, 2002 to provide a host of complementary treatments to restore the immune system and to provide comprehensive and holistic health care. The center has grown since its early beginnings and now provides its services through a network of three Immune Recovery Clinics. The basic philosophy of the Foundation is that a common concern in all health challenges is a suppressed immune system. A highly motivated team of medical doctors, nurses, and other health care practitioners specialize in treating acute and chronic medical conditions, using both conventional and non-allopathic modalities on an out-patient basis. What follows is an interview with the CEO of the Immune Recovery Institute, Dr. Bradford:

Ricardo: How does alternative medicine complement conventional medicine in America?

Dr. Bradford: We need to keep in mind that alternative medicine is a term that is dated and complementary is a better choice of words. Anyone that is using non-allopathic or complementary medicine must keep in mind that it is exactly what it is does, it complements all of the allopathic treatment modalities that have the science behind it. It will allow you to modify or decrease the allopathic treatment modalities without the side effects that are normally seen.

Ricardo: What would be the health status of Americans, in general, if there were no legalized non-allopathic medicine?

Dr. Bradford: We now are very, very cost conscience. We are also interested in educating patients about self-care and taking part in their treatment modalities. When you educate a patient and they know more about their disease disorder, the first thing they will want to do is self-treat. I think there must be more education on how they are going to self-treat. For example, those who have migraine headaches do not need to go to the emergency room, they can learn about their body, and what they can or cannot take as far as medicine is concern. On the other hand, if they have a family history of hepatitis, they should be educated that they should not take Tylenol because of the potential damage to their liver. Educating oneself about the body is most important. We need to educate the consumer about complementary medicine and procedures the same way we have educated individuals about diet and cholesterol to prevent heart disease and other chronic disorders.

Ricardo: What is the difference between conventional and non-allopathic medicine?

Dr. Bradford: Conventional medicine has the advantage of research that has been conducted in the laboratory and replicated. Complementary medicine is more anecdotal and does not have statistical data to back it up. Consequently, it doesn't fit into the standards of care conventional medicine has adopted.

Ricardo: In what ways are conventional medical approaches superior to non-allopathic?

Dr. Bradford: I think that individuals who have an acute disorder probably should be treated with conventional medicine, if all things are equal. For example, when someone has just been diagnosed with cancer and surgery is an option then perhaps surgery is the best way to go. The supportive or maintenance treatment thereafter is where complementary medicine has a role.

Ricardo: In what ways are non-allopathic approaches superior to conventional medicine?

Dr. Bradford: Again, using cancer as an example, when the allopathic medical modalities have failed the patient (i.e. chemo, radiation, or surgery) then certainly complementary medicine may be the only choice available.

Ricardo: What is responsible for the growth of non-allopathic medicine in America?

Dr. Bradford: Again, education—it's not the stone age, it's not snake oil. There have been fewer studies done on most alternative treatment modalities mainly because the products used are natural. For example, vitamin C has been shown to cause death to cancer cells. There have not been very many studies published about vitamin C. Vitamin C cannot be patented because it is a natural drug, so big Pharma isn't interested in doing the studies. Vitamin C has been found to complement radiation therapy, it also complements some chemotherapy. Vitamin C was discovered to make cells more sensitive to chemotherapy drugs and to radiation.

Ricardo: Is there tension between conventional and non-allopathic medical practitioners?

Dr. Bradford: Yes, there certainly is tension between these health care providers. The reason is that here is a standard of care established by the American Medical Association and the schools that teach conventional medicine use this model. Everyone is trained to look at the statistics, the history, the physic exams and the treatment modalities. There isn't enough scientific data out there on alternative treatment modalities and the funding isn't there for the necessary research. Conventional practitioners want to see the science, they want to see the data, the clinical trials, and the empirical results—that is why there is tension.

Ricardo: Given the options available and the money spent on health care in America why aren't Americans healthier than they are, generally speaking?

Dr. Bradford: We need to go back to basics. If you eat a healthy diet, get enough sleep (seven to eight hours a night) and exercise, I think we would be healthier just doing those things alone. Now we are exposed to toxins and environmental hazards every day. Things that we drink and eat, and the way we prepare our foods can weaken our immune system.

Ricardo: How do you see the health care landscape, in terms of conventional and non-allopathic medicine in the next twenty years?

Dr. Bradford: Certainly with the web, I think that twenty years from now we are going to see more people taking more responsibility for their treatment. A lot more people will take responsibility for their future and that of generations to come. A lot of things we are doing from a conventional medicine standpoint will not be the same twenty years from now. I think there will be more health care extenders providing health care and they will not be medical doctors. There will be other health care providers extending the work of the traditional medical doctor. It may take twenty years for the change and it might certainly reduce the financial burden.

Chapter Fourteen

*Silver Nanoparticles, HIV Treatment, and Uposh

Uposh is an anagram that stands for Uniform Picoscalar Oligodymanic Silver Hydrosol. This treatment protocol is used to treat acute and chronic infectious processes. Uposh is a modern application of a treatment with a long history. It is currently in use to address a wide range of health conditions, including HIV/AIDS.

It has been estimated that acquired immune deficiency syndrome (AIDS) has killed more than 25 million people since it was first recognized in 1981. Globally there are approximately 33.3 million people currently living with the human immunodeficiency virus (HIV), as of 2009.

There is currently no cure for AIDS or vaccines to prevent this disease. The treatment protocols generally considered to be most effective typically involve two or three different anti-retroviral drugs used in combination. The use of antiretroviral drugs has reduced the morbidity and mortality associated with AIDS, however, a significant number of HIV infections have become resistant to antiretroviral treatment.

The use of alternative treatment approaches has been a widespread practice since the existence of HIV/AID was first reported by the Centers for Disease Control of Atlanta. The cost and the politics of access to antiretroviral therapies, appears to have encouraged the use of these other treatment approaches. Denial and stigma associated with HIV/AIDS are factors which have obstructed testing

---

* This article was condensed for readability. The reference list articles were used to develop the original article. The original is an unpublished manuscript.

for HIV and the use of antiretroviral drugs. The effectiveness of alternative therapies has not been established, despite widespread use by people living with HIV/AIDS. When used in conjunction with conventional antiretroviral therapies, alternative approaches are often referred to as complementary treatments.

Four different types of silver products are on the market for use in treating microbes. Colloidal silver products are colloidal suspensions of silver particles in water. Particles in silver colloid are typically 0.01 to 0.001 microns in diameter and carry a positive electrical charge. The one type of colloidal silver is called electro-colloidal silver made either by electro-arc method in de-ionized water or the low voltage electrolysis method in distilled water. Concentrations are usually between 3-5 ppm but sometimes as high as 100 ppm. Mild silver protein chemically binds microscopic particles of silver to a protein molecule and is usually found in concentrations between 50-500 ppm. Silver salts dissolve in water and usually contain elements other that silver. They can be made either chemically or electro-chemically. Concentrations range between 50-500 ppm. Powdered silver is made when a pure silver wire is rapidly disintegrated by high voltage electricity. This dust is added to water or added to salves and creams for topical use. Silver products behave differently in the body and in laboratory tests. Dosage and quality vary considerably, and regulatory standards do not currently exist.

Previous investigation with HIV/AID patients made use of mild silver protein and silver oxide. Nano-silver is considered to be more efficient because a greater amount of cell surface area coverage is possible with nanoparticles. Further assessment is needed to expand knowledge regarding the role of silver nanoparticles in HIV/AIDS treatment protocols.

A number of medical researchers and practitioners have called for new drugs to combat HIV, because the replication process of the HIV virus results in numerous mutations, which can make the virus resistant to antiretroviral drugs. Research suggests that oligodynamic silver (Ag+) may be a viable alternative treatment for HIV treatment since silver has anti-microbial properties that selectively targets and kills rapidly proliferating single celled organisms such as bacterial, viral, fungi, protozoa and other pathogens, while normal tissues remain unaffected.

The virotoxicity of silver particles against a wide range of bacteria, viruses, fungi and other microbes has received a considerable amount of scientific investigation. The collective authoritative medical literature documents the efficacy of silver particles against over 24 viruses. The list of viruses exhibiting silver cytotoxicity includes HIV. Empirical investigation suggests that silver is an effective antiviral agent that may be useful in treatment and management of HIV/AIDS and other major diseases such as hepatitis B and hepatitis C.

Researchers have demonstrated effects of silver nanoparticles in disturbing the replication of HIV viruses, however additional human trials are needed.

Toxicity

Reports on toxic effects of silver on the human body are mixed. Some negative side-effects of silver treatment have been observed such as Jarisch-Herxheimer-like reactions. This reaction is characterized by severe chills, muscle aches, headache, fever, increased heart rate, and increased respiration. Jarisch-Herxheimer-like reactions decreased with repeated infusions and researchers generally found silver treatment to be safe and effective.

Other medical practitioners have found that long-term use of silver deposits metallic silver under the skin, causing a permanent skin discoloration known as Argyria, which is carcinogenic. Medical practitioners report that when silver administrations are kept within specified limits, and liver function is monitored, silver is a safe, effective anti-microbial agent that appears to decrease HIV viral load and improve immune function in AIDS patients.

The key to silver toxicity is particle size. When silver nanoparticles are used, toxicity problems are averted. The diameter of the capillary lumen is 4-9 microns, as such the body has no problem excreting silver particles. That is why there has not been a single case of Argyria from a properly manufactured modern day colloidal sliver product. The cases of Argyria reported in the 1920's and 1930's resulted because the technology of the day was unable to produce a colloidal silver product with a small enough particle size.

Colloidal silver and particle size

Nanotechnology is at the cutting edge among today's scientific and technological advances. Nanotechnology has allowed scientist to engineer the properties of materials by controlling characteristics such as particle size. Silver nanoparticles have received considerable attention in medicine because of their ability to enhance surface coverage, with reduced toxicity considerations. For example, particles that have been dispersed into sizes below 10 microns will yield greater coverage over the surface area of cells, than particles above 10 microns in size. The nanoparticle also has an enhanced ability to react with its environment due to its high surface area. Particulate surface area is the single most important property of colloids. Surface area increases as the concentration of metal particles increases. Surface area also increases as the particle size decreases. The higher the particle surface area, the more effective the colloid.

Ultrasound is one method used to achieve liquids composed of nano-size particles. Ultrasonic processors are used to reduce material slurries, dispersions and emulsions into nano-size particles. The ultrasound method uses cavitation forces to reduce particle size. Cavitation is the formation, growth, and implosive collapse of bubbles in a liquid. Sonicating liquids at high-frequency or low intensity can cause cavitation. While there are a number of methods such as rotor stator mixers, piston homogenizers, gear pumps, beat mills, colloid mills and ball mills, ultrasound is an efficient, well-established method for producing nano-size dispersions and emulsions.

History of Silver Use

Silver is nontoxic to humans if properly used and it has a long history of medical and public health use dating back 6000 years. There are reports of silvers use in treating wounds by the ancient Egyptians and Macedonians. The Druids lined their drinking bottles with silver and the ancient Greeks ate from silver utensils. Silver has been used to purify water and to treat infections. It has also been used to sterilize surgical equipment and as plates in the surgical repair of bones. Silver has been used to treat hundreds of ailments including syphilis, eczema, pneumonia, tuberculosis, pleurisy, gonorrhea, leg ulcers and impetigo, from around 1893 until antibiotics came into common use. Silver is classified as a multivalent metallic oxide rather than a heavy metal.

There is evidence to suggest that nano particle silver may provide therapeutic benefit in certain cases of HIV/AIDS. Further research is needed to determine the efficacy of colloidal silver and its range of applicability.

References

Bean P. New drug targets for HIV. Clinical Infectious Diseases. 2005; 41: S96-S100.

Bean P. HIV genetic mutations causing resistance to the new drug T-20: recent findings. *Am Clin Lab*. 2002; 21:15-16.

Gordon E, Holtorf K. A promising cure for URTI pandemics, including H5N1 and SARS: Has the final solution to the coming plagues been discovered? (Part II). Townsend Letter: The Examiner of Alternative Medicine. Available at: *http://www.gordonresearch.com*. Accessed November 25, 2007.

Antelman MS. Method of curing AIDS with tetrasilver tetroxide molecular crystal devices. *USPTO # 5,676,977*, October 14, 1997.

Dean W, Mitchell M, Lugo VW, et. al. Reduction of Viral Load in AIDS Patients with Intravenous Mild Silver Protein: Three Case Reports. *Clinical Practice of Alternative Medicine*. 2001; 2(1): 48-53.

Oka H, et al. Inactivation of enveloped viruses by a silver-thiosulfate complex. *Metal Based Drugs*. 1994;1(5-6):511.

Hussain S, et al. Cystine protects Na, K-ATPase and isolated human lymphocytes from silver toxicity. *Biochem., Biophys Res Comm*. 1992;189:1444-1449.

Making History: Curing HIV/AIDS with nanotechnology. Available at: *www.enkidumagazin.com/eventos/aidsinculture/abstracts*. Accessed November 27, 2007.

Fields CB, et al. Method for treating blood borne viral pathogens such as immunodeficiency virus. *United States Patent No. 6,066,489*. 2000; May 23.

Elechiguerra, JL, Burt, JL, Morones, JR, et al. Interaction of silver nanoparticles with HIV-1. *Journal of Nanobiotechnology*. 2005; 3:6. Available at: *www.jnanobiotechnology.com/content* Accessed December 15, 2006.

Zhong-Yin Z, Reardon I M, Hui JO, O'Connell KL, Poorman RA, Tomasselli AG, et al. Zinc inhibition of renin and the protease from human immunodeficiency virus type 1. *Biochemistry*. 1991; 30(36):8717-8721.

Bradley JS. *Clusters and Colloids: From theory to applications*. In Clusters and Colloids: From Theory to Applications. Edited by: Schmid GE. Weinheim, VCH:1994; 459-536.

Deng H, Liu R, Ellmeier W, Choe S, Unutmaz D, Burkhart M, et al. Identification of a major co-receptor for primary isolates of HIV-1. *Nature*. 1996; 381(20): 661-666.

Chackerian B, Long EM, Luciw PA, Overbaugh J. Human immunodeficiency virus type 1 coreceptors participate in postentry stags in the virus replication cycle and function in simian immunodeficiency virus infection. *J Virol*. 1997; 71: 3932-3939.

Kaltenbach JP, Kaltenbach MH, Lyons WB: Nigrosin as a dye for differentiating live and dead ascites cells* I. *Exp Cell Res*. 1958; 15:112-117.

Mafune F, Kohno J.Takeda Y, et al. *J. Phys. Chem. B*. 2000; 104: 8333.

Eberle J, Seibi R, *J. Virol. Methods*. 1992; 40: 347.

Sun RW, Chen R, Chung NP, et al. Silver nanoparticles fabricated in Hepes buffer exhibit cytoprotective activities toward HIV-1 infected cells. *Chem. Comm*. 2005; 40: 5059-5061.

US Patent Claiming CURE for AIDS (USP # 5,336,499). Available at: *www.rexresearch.com/antelman/silverox.htm*. Accessed December 14, 2006.

Hielscher T. Ultrasonic production of nano-size dispersions and emulsions. Available at: *http://www.hielscher.com/ultrasonic/nano_00.htm*. Accessed November 15, 2007.

Cloete A. *All you need to know about Colloidal Silver*. Available at: http://www.revivalnook.co.za. Accessed October 15, 2007.

Feng QL, Wu J, Chen GQ, et al. A mechanistic study of the antibacterial effect of silver ions on Escherichia Coli and Staphylococcus aureus. *J Biomed Mater Res*. 2000; 52: 662-668.

Liau SY, Read DC, Pugh WJ, et al. Interaction of silver-nitrate with readily identifiable groups—relationship to the antibacterial action of silver ions. *Lett Appl Microbio*. 1997; 25:279-283.

Lok C, Ho C, Chen R, et al. Proteomic analysis of the mode of anti-bacterial action of silver nanoparticles. *Journal of Proteome Research*. 2006; 5:916-924.

Berger TJ, Spadaro JA, Bierman R, et al. Antifungal properties of electrically generated metallic ions. *Antimicrobial Agents and Chemotherapy*. 1976; 10(5). 856-860.

Farber P. The Micro Silver bullet? CA: Professional Physicians Publishing & Health Services. 1996.

Chalder T, Berelowitz G, Pawlikowska T, et al. Development of a fatigue scale. *Journal of Psychosomatic Research*. 1993; 37(2) 147-153.

Schwarzer R. Self-efficacy in the adoption and maintenance of health behaviors: Theoretical approaches and a new model. In R.Schwarzer (Ed.), *Self-efficacy: Thought control of action* (pp.217-242). Washington, DC: Hemisphere. 1992.

Wikipedia:The Free Encyclopedia. Available at: *http://en.wikipedia.org/wiki/HIV*. Accessed November 15, 2007.

Palella F J, Delaney K M, Moorman AC, et al. Declining morbidity and mortality among patients with advanced human immunodeficiency virus infection. *N. Engl. J. Med* 1998; 338 (13): 853-860.

Brenner BG, Turner D, Wainberg MA. HIV-1 drug resistance: can we overcome? *Expert Opin Biol Ther*. 2002; 2:751-761.

Shanta, TR. *AIDS-HIV: A perscription for survival*. GA: International Publishing House. 1991.

Watson J. Scientists, activists sue South Africa's AIDS 'denialists'. *Nat. Med.* 2006;12 (1): 6.

Baleta A. South Africa's AIDS activists accuse government of murder. *Lancet* 2003; 361(9363):1105.

Cohen J. South Africa's new enemy. *Science*. 2000; 288 (5474): 2168-2170.

Mills E, Wu P, Ernst E. Complementary therapies for the treatment of HIV: in search of the evidence. *Int. J. STD AIDS*. 2005;16 (6): 395-403.

Chapter Fifteen

*Affirmative Acton Policy in Medical School Admissions

Title VII of the Civil Rights Act of 1964 was enacted by Congress to enforce the doctrine of equal employment opportunity under the law. Legislative action was deemed necessary to counteract the ill effects of long-term institutional racism and discrimination. President Lyndon Johnson signed the Civil Rights Act into law in 1964. Title VII was later amended and applied to all private employers of 15 or more persons, all educational institutions, state and local governments, apprentice programs and employment agencies.[1] Programs that grew out of this Civil Rights legislation were dubbed as *affirmative action programs*; the scope of affirmative action includes the rights of women, as well as those of racial and ethnic minorities and other groups that were traditionally under-represented in the workforce.[2]

Affirmative action programs have been challenged from their inception and such challenges are growing. One popular argument against affirmative action legislation is that the resulting programs give unfair advantage to underqualified individuals, therefore representing unfair reverse discrimination against applicants who would have been selected if merit were the definitive criteria. In a 2003 address to the nation, President George W. Bush asserted that the University of Michigan's affirmative action admissions policies were "fundamentally flawed" and "unconstitutional." He stated, "the Michigan policies amount to a quota system that unfairly rewards or penalizes perspective

---

*   This article is reprinted from the Journal of Health Care for the Poor and Underserved 2005 Fall; 16 (1): 12-18.

[sic] students, based solely on their race." In June 2003, the U.S. Supreme Court upheld affirmative action legislation by permitting race to be considered as a factor in college admissions. However, in a second ruling, the court ruled against the automatic awarding of points based on an individual's race.

In a number of states (including Texas, Louisiana and Mississippi [1996]; California [1997]; Washington [1998]; and Florida [2000]) court rulings, state-wide propositions and/or state legislation have banned affirmative action programs. Significant drops in minority student enrollment subsequently materialized in those states. In 1998, the number of black, Mexican American, Native American, and mainland Puerto Rican medical school applicants dropped 11% nationally and the number of entrants from these under-represented groups dropped 7.4%.[4]

The number of minority students admitted to the University of California at Berkeley dropped more than 50% after affirmative action was banned. One year after affirmative action was challenged, the University of Texas Law School reduced the number of African Americans enrolled by 88%. Without affirmative action, 80% fewer minorities would have been enrolled in U.S. medical schools in 1996, according to data released by the Association of American Medical Colleges.[5] Importantly, on June 23, 2003, the U.S. Supreme Court upheld the University of Michigan Law School's admission policy, ruling that race may be considered along with many other factors when higher education al institutions select students because doing so speaks to "compelling interest in obtaining the educational benefits that flow from a diverse student body." This decision, *Grutter v. Bollinger*, also effectively over-ruled major portions of the 1996 ruling of the Court of Appeals for the Fifth Circuit in *Hopwood v. Texas* that had brought about the cessation of affirmative action in admissions in Texas, Mississippi and Louisiana.

There is still a need for profound and drastic changes in many areas of American society to improve the condition and quality of life for all Americans. Affirmative action is one belated effort to address the dire need to remedy the economic and social conditions rooted in racial slavery. Thirty plus years after the adoption of affirmation action legislation, minorities remain grossly underrepresented among the population of physicians. For example, by 1983-84 minority student enrollment in US medical schools reached 15% and enrollment of underrepresented minorities (blacks, Mexican American, Native Americans and mainland Puerto Ricans) rose to 11.1 %.[6] In 1995, these underrepresented minority groups made up 21% of the American population but accounted for only 12% of medical student enrollment. In 2003, there were 819, 000 physicians and surgeons in the United States, of which blacks and Hispanics constituted 5.0% and 4.7%, respectively.[7]

A real need for physicians to serve out-of-hospital populations still exists, as noted by the World Health Organization at its Edinburgh, Scotland meeting in

1988.[8] The World Conference on Medical Education of the World Federation for Medical Education stated unequivocally that training based almost exclusively in tertiary care hospitals will not adequately prepare medical students for roles in community-oriented primary care.[8] Subsequent declarations by various health care organizations have articulated the need to expand the pool of community-based primary care physicians through increased recruitment efforts.[9] This essay is intended to champion recruitment procedures that expand the pool of community-oriented and primary care physicians from underrepresented populations while questioning an overreliance on current applicant selection strategies.

Admission into medical school generally hinges on a formulation with two primary factors, the Medical College Admissions Test (MCAT) and college grade point average (GPA). Secondary selection criteria, which include a variety of demographics such as race and geographic region, are frequently also considered. Relevant factors are often weighted to form a total Index. However, analysis of court cases where selection procedures have been challenged suggests that after selection criteria have been determined and weights assigned, at the end of the day, a cut-off MCAT test score is the primary admissions criteria. [10,11] This is so even though many studies of undergraduate students have found that college GPAs are better single predictors of future academic achievement, regardless of the student's socioeconomic or racial category.[12]

The heavy emphasis on standardized tests as selection criteria makes obvious the need for evidence that the tests are valid indicators for all groups. However, there is in fact evidence to suggest that the MCAT does a poor job of predicting success during clinical training and during actual practice as a physician.[13] There is very little evidence to suggest that the MCAT and other cognitive ability tests are reliable predictors of medical school achievement as measured by grades and National Board of Medical Examiners examinations.[14] The magnitude of achievement correlations found is generally in the 0.30s and 0.40s. Although scholars consider this adequate, these figures suggest that the standard predictors account for only approximately 9% to 16% percent of the variation in medical school achievement, leaving 84% to 91% of the variation in achievement due to unknown or unmeasured factors.[13] This would not be a strong defense of the MCAT or college GPA if challenged in court.

Research was been conducted in an effort to identity the incremental effects of other predictors of academic performance in medical school. Hojat and co-workers[15] examined effects of selected psychosocial measures, beyond the effects of conventional measures (such as the MCAT and GPA). Eleven psychosocial measures (such as depression, external locus of control, sociability, neuroticism, and self-esteem) were included in the study. The findings demonstrated that the psychosocial measures increased the magnitude of the correlations between predictors and criterion 14 % beyond what was achieved by the conventional measures alone.[15]

A growing body of empirical evidence suggests that for minority applicants, standardized test scores measure constructs different from those measured for majority applicants. Furthermore, researchers have found weak relationships between standardized tests and performance on various criteria. Some have found no relationship, and others have found a negative relationship between standardized test scores and performance for Blacks but a positive relationship for whites.[16-19] Although these findings, which are based on the performance of undergraduates, cannot be generalized to black and Hispanic medical school applicants, they suggest that further research is needed to identify why these students perform poorly on standardized tests.

Historically, courts have focused on examining psychometric studies of differential validity in order to determine the fairness of a given test for blacks and whites. The effort has been made to determine if a test was a valid predictor of performance for different racial groups. Many statistical procedures or models exist for how to go about determining differential validity. Generally speaking, differential validity asks the question, "are the correlation coefficients representing the relationship between the predictor (generally a standardized test) and the criterion (a measure of performance such as grade point average) essentially the same for the different racial groups under consideration or are the correlations significantly different?" Experts do not agree on what constitute a biased or a fair test and various models with varying implications (the number of applicants selected from the various racial groups varies based on the model used) have been set forth as standards for test evaluation.[20-22]

Research has now shifted from evaluating test bias to designing selection strategies that enhance fairness. This includes the search for additional criteria for selecting qualified applicants. An important development is the use of expected utility analysis.[23] This decision strategy provides a tool for assessing the usefulness of various selection approaches. Utility analysis makes explicit the value judgments implicit in the statistical models used to make decisions. This approach requires researchers to specify the underlying social values inherent in the statistical procedures used and to reconcile the statistical procedures with social values such as increasing diversity and providing equality of opportunity.[23] Many scholars have argued that a utility function would be served by training more minority physicians, because they would be likely to bring needed services to traditionally underserved areas.[4,24] This prediction has been borne out. Investigators found that minority graduates tend to practice in areas federally designated as experiencing shortages of medical personnel. For example, Davidson and associates,[24] examined the medical practices of minorities who graduated from seven California medical schools and found that 53% of minority graduates were likely to serve in areas of shortage, whereas 26 % of majority physicians served in areas of shortage. In another study analyzing data from a 1987 National Medical Expenditure survey of the total non-institutionalized US population (n=15,081), it was found that 14.4 % of adult Americans identified a nonwhite physician as the source of their care.[25] Minority medical graduates are four times more likely than whites to practice in underserved areas, according to the Association of American Medical Colleges.[4]

It has been reported that blacks, on average, do not perform as well on standardized tests as whites.[26-30] A possible, if doubtful, inference from this is that blacks are not as intelligent as whites. However, such an inference masks facts about unequal employment and educational opportunities that are central to understanding the problematic test results; the problematic inference invites the reasoner to find and explanation in individual cognitive differences while ignoring the structural societal factors that differentially affect different races. One way to increase the validity of MCAT scores for ethnic and racial minorities lies in building the pipeline of underrepresented minority students through high school and college. In doing so, it is critical to note that cognitive ability testing has already badly weakened this pipeline. Of particular concern is the choice of cognitive abilities deemed important enough to test. The MCAT is said to access thought processes, as well as knowledge of science, but the range of thought processes tested by the MCAT is small relative to the range identified by cognitive scientists.

Admission tests for medical school should measure the cognitive abilities that enable an individual to do well in school and the characteristics required of good physicians. What is needed is a conceptual model that links the various cognitive abilities needed for successes in medical school to the skills and abilities needed to be a good physician. These cognitive abilities should be operationally defined as measurable characteristics relevant to the life experiences of racial and ethnic minorities as well as those of majority group members. Research is needed that identifies race-related factors that contribute to poor test performance which can be corrected. Potential factors for investigation include such variables as test anxiety, test-wiseness, stereotypical threat, motivational differences, racial/ethnic identity, linguistic bias, and academic self-efficacy, to name only a few. Once this research is completed, operational models can be proposed for how one might formally address the problem.

Those who argue for merit-based selection make the assumption that our science of measurement is objective and free from cultural bias. However, until social scientists reach some form of consensus regarding an adequate definition for constructs such as cognitive ability, intelligence and scholastic achievement, tests designed to measure these characteristics will lack construct validity. Most standardized tests that measure the cognitive ability of medical school applicants emphasize the measurement of a relative small number of facilities involving science problem solving, reading and quantitative skills. However, other identified forms of intelligence such as creative problem solving, social skills, emotional intelligence, and integrative thinking, are not currently assessed. We are currently operating as if standardized tests measure whatever the test label say they measure and that what is being tested is measured adequately and fairly for all groups. To improve this system, In addition to standard measurements of the abilities that enable students to do well in school (reading, writing, and solving quantitative problems), ability testing for prospective medical students must also be linked to the likely quality of their performance as physicians. This requires rigorous analyses of what leads to success as a physician in all areas, from the research lab to the patient's bedside. Thorough-going job analysis can provide the basic information necessary for the development of additional selection criteria.

The wheels of social science will continue to turn, but they will never be free of political and social agendas. Affirmative action legislation has been interpreted and reinterpreted, testing the boundaries set by its original intent and substance. Through all of the turmoil, affirmative action policy remains an important legal tool for addressing some of the valued social goals of our culturally diverse society. Among these goals are training members of underrepresented minority groups as physicians and increasing the number of physicians providing community-oriented health care, goals that experience tells us are linked.

References

1. U.S. Equal Employment Opportunity Commission (EEOC. Affirmative action and equal employment: A guidebook for employers (Volume 1). Washington, D. C.: U.S. Equal Employment Opportunity Commission; January, 1974.

2. Dulles FR. The civil rights commission:1957-1965. Ann Arbor: Michigan State University, 1968.

3. Office of the Press Secretary of the White House of President George W. Bush. President Bush Discusses Michigan Affirmative Action Case: Remarks by the President on the Michigan Affirmative Action Case. Washington, D. C.: The Roosevelt Room, the White House, January 15, 2003. Available from URl: www.whitehouse.gov/news/releases/2003/01.

4. Wilson, JF. The backlash against affirmative action: With minority admissions falling, educators consider new options. American College of Physicians Observer 1998 Jan;18(1): 1, 14-15. Available from http://www.acponline.org./journals/news/jan98/backlash.htm

5. Association of American Medical Colleges (AAMC). Minority Students in Medical Education: Facts and Figures, Volumes VII-XII. Washington, D. C.: Association of American Medical Colleges; 1993-2003.

6. Davidson RC, Montoya, R. The distribution of services to the underserved: A comparison of Minority and Majority Medical Graduates in California. The West J Med 1987 Jan;146:114-117.

7. Bureau of Labor Statistics. Office of Employment and Unemployment Statistics. Current Population Survey, 2004. http://www.bls.gov/cps/home.htm.

8. Metcalfe DH. The Edinburgh declaration. Fam Pract 1989 Sept; 6(3): 165-7.

9. Smilkstein G. Designing a Curriculum For Training Community-Responsive Physicians. J Health Care Poor Underserved 1990 Fall; 1 (2): 237-242.

10. Hopwood v. The State of Texas, 1996

11. Podberesky v. Kirwin, 1995.

12. McCornack RL. Bias in the validity of predicted college grades in four ethnic minority groups. Educational and Psychological Measurement 1983; 43: 517-522.

13. McGaghie, W.C. Perspectives on Medical School Admission. Academic medicine 1990 March;65(3): 136-139.

14. Johnson, D.G. Physicians in the Making. San Francisco, California: Jossey-Bass, 1983.

15. Hojat, M., Robeson, M., Damjanov, I., et al. Students' psychosocial characteristics as predictors of academic performance in medical school. Academic Medicine 1993 Aug;68(8): 635-7.

16. Vars FE, Bowen WG. Scholastic Aptitude Test scores, race, and academic performance in selective colleges and universities. In: C. Jencks and M. Phillips, eds. The Black-White test score gap. Washington, DC: Brokings Institution,1998.

17. Bowen, WG, Bok, D. The shape of the river: Long term consequences of considering race in college and university admissions,1998.

18. Scott R, Shaw M. Black and White performance in graduate school and policy implications of the use of Graduate Record Examination scores in admissions. Journal of Negro Education 1985; 54: 14-23.

19. Lawlor S, Richman S, Richman C. The validity of using the SAT as a criterion for Black and White students' admission to college. College Student Journal 1994; 31 (4): 507-515.

20. Arvey, RD. Fairness in Selecting Employees. Mass: Addison-Wesley Publishing Company,1979.

21. Schmeiser, C.B., Ferguson, R.L. Performance of black and white students on test materials containing content based on black and white cultures. Journal of Educational Measurement 1978;15 (3): 193-200.

22. Cole, N.S. Bias in Testing. American Psychologist 1981; 36 (10): 1067-77.

23. Anastasi, A. Urbina, S. Psychological Testing. New Jersey: Prentice Hall, 1997.

24. Davidson, R.C., Lewis, E.L., Affirmative action and other special consideration admissions at the University of California, Davis, School of Medicine. JAMA. 1997; 274: 1153-1158.

25. Moy, E., Bartman B.A. Physician race and care of minority and medically indigent patients. JAMA. 1995; 173: 1515-1520.

26. Jensen AR. Bias in mental testing. New York: The Free Press, 1980.

27. Herrnstein B, Murray C. The bell curve: intelligence and class structure in American life. New York: Simon & Schuster, The Free Press, 1996.

28. Lynn R. Racial and ethnic differences in intelligence in the U.S. on the Differential Ability Scale. Personality and Individual Differences 1996; 20: 271-3.

29. Williams WM, Ceci SJ. Are Americans becoming more or less alike? Trends in race, class, and ability differences in intelligence. Am Psychol 1997; 52 (11): 1226-35.

30. Flynn, JR. Searching for justice: the discovery of IQ gains over time. Am Psychol 1999; 54 (1): 5-20.

Chapter Sixteen

Karmu's Healing Herbs and How to Use Them

Aloe (Aloe socotrina) is a cathartic, stomachic, aromatic, and emmenagogue. Promotes menstruation. Will expel pinworms after several doses. This herb is used in many cathartics to help clean out the colon. To assist with moving the bowels, take: 1 oz. powdered buckthorn bark, 1 oz. powdered rhubarb root, 1 oz. powdered mandrake root, ¼ oz. powdered aloe, and 1 oz. powdered calamus root. Start with ¼ tsp. of this mixture and adjust the dosage according to individual needs.

Aloe is one of the finest colon and body cleansers—cleanses morbid matter from the stomach, liver, kidneys, spleen, bladder and colon. Can be used in any case where a laxative is needed—does not gripe, and is very healing and soothing. Aloes may be used for any kind of external sore, and is an excellent remedy for piles and hemorrhoids. Add one heaping teaspoonful of powder to a pint of water and strain. Adding two tsp. of borac acid is beneficial and will help keep the mixture from becoming sour.

Ginseng (Pannax quinquefolia) is a demulcent, stomachic, and stimulant. Ginseng helps promote appetite and is useful in digestive disturbances. When flavored, makes an agreeable drink for colds, chest troubles, and coughs. Good for stomach troubles, constipation, lung troubles, and inflammation of the urinary tract.

GOLDEN SEAL (*Hydrastis canadensis*) is a laxative, tonic, alterative, detergent, opthalmicum, antiperiodic, aperients, diuretic, antiseptic, and deobstruent. One of the best substitutes for quinine. Is an excellent remedy for colds, grippe, stomach troubles, and liver troubles. Benefits mucous membranes and tissues that it comes in contact with. Good for open sores, inflammations, eczema, ringworm, erysipelas, or many skin diseases. Golden seal tea is made by steeping one teaspoonful in a pint of boiling water for 20 minutes. Can be used as a wash—clean the skin with hydrogen peroxide, sprinkle the powered root on the skin, and cover.

Taken in small but frequent doses, it will allay nausea during pregnancy. Steep a tsp. in a pint of boiling water for 20 minutes, stir well, let settle, and pour off the liquid. Take 6 tablespoons a day. Will equalize circulation. Combined with skullcap and red cayenne pepper will greatly relieve and strengthen the heart. It has no superior when combined with myrrh (1 part golden seal to ¼ part myrrh) for ulcerated stomach, duodenum, and dyspepsia. Especially good for enlarged tonsils and mouth sores. Smoker's sores (caused by holding a pipe in the mouth), will heal after a few applications of powder to the sores. Golden seal combined with myrrh and cayenne is an excellent remedy for diphtheria, tonsillitis, and other throat troubles. Good for chronic catarrh of the intestines and all catarrhal conditions. Will improve appetite and aid digestion. Combined with skullcap and hops it makes an excellent tonic for spinal nerves. Very good for spinal meningitis, skin eruptions, scarlet fever and smallpox.

To cure pyorrhea or sore gums, put some of the tea in a cup, dip toothbrush in solution, and thoroughly brush teeth and gums. For any nose trouble, pour some tea into the palm of the hand and snuff up the nose.

Golden seal is useful in typhoid fever, gonorrhea, leucorrhea and syphilis. For bladder troubles, have a nurse or physician inject golden seal solution into the bladder with a rubber catheter immediately after the bladder has been emptied, and retain as long as possible—repeating 2 or 3 times a day.

Two parts golden seal combined with one part wild alum, taken internally, is a laxative and excellent remedy for bowel and bladder troubles. Good for piles, hemorrhoids, and prostate gland. When combined with equal parts red clover blossoms, yellow dock, and dandelion it has a wonderful effect on the gall bladder, kidneys, liver, and pancreas. Combined with peach leaves, queen of the meadow, cleaver and corn silk, it is a reliable remedy for Bright's disease and diabetes.

It is an excellent remedy for the eyes if the eyelids are granulated or there is film over the eyes: steep a tsp. of golden seal and one of boric acid in a pint of boiling water, stir well, let cool, and pour off the liquid. Put a tablespoonful of this remedy in a half cup of water and bathe the eyes, using an eye dropper or eye cup. If used a little too strong, it will smart a little, but there is no harm done.

Take ¼ tsp. of golden seal dissolved in a glass of hot water immediately on arising, and one hour before the noon and evening meals. Or, steep a teaspoon in a pint of boiling water, stir well, let cool, pour the liquid off and take a tablespoonful 4 to 6 times a day. Children should take less doses, according to age.

Chronic catarrh of the intestines can be helped with golden seal. Produces healing in ulceration of the mucous lining of the rectum and is effective in hemorrhage of the rectum. A remedy for chronic and intermittent malarial poisoning or enlarged spleen due to malaria.

ROSEMARY (Rosemarinus officinalis) is a stimulant, antispasmodic, emmenagogue, tonic, astringent, diaphoretic, carminative, nervine, aromatic, and cephalic. Leaves and flower are used. Good for colds, colic, nervous conditions, and nervous headaches. Rosemary should be taken warm for these complaints. Good as wash for mouth, gums, bad breath and sore throat. The leaves are used for flavoring foods. Rosemary oil is used as a perfume for ointments and liniments. An excellent ingredient for shampoos. Rosemary aids digestion, coughs, consumption, mental imbalance, and strengthens eyes.

SASSAFRAS (Sassafras officianale) is aromatic, stimulant, alterative, diaphoretic, and diuretic. The bark of the root is used. Purifies blood and cleanses entire system. Good for flavoring herbs that have a disagreeable taste. Useful as a stomach and bowel tonic and relieves gas. Taken warm, sassafras is an excellent remedy for spasms. Sassafras is a useful treatment for colic, skin diseases and eruptions. Good wash for inflamed eyes. Sassafras is very good for kidneys, bladder, varicose ulcers, chest and throat troubles. Oil of sassafras is excellent for toothaches.

SNAKEROOT (Aristolochia serpentaria) is a stimulant, tonic, and diaphoretic. Dried rhizomes and roots are used. In the United States, it is grown primarily in central and southern states. Small doses will promote appetite, and tone digestive organs. Too large a dose will produce nausea, and griping pains in bowels. Recommended for intermittent fevers—may be used as an adjunct to quinine. In strong doses produces increased arterial action, diaphoresis and diuresis. Snakeroot excels in eruptive fever where the eruption is tardy, or in the typhoid stage where a strong stimulant cannot be used. Snakeroot helps to promote recovery in chronic forms of gouty inflammation. Excessive boiling impairs its virtues. A cold infusion is useful in convalescence from acute diseases. Dosage: powder root: 10 to 30 grains. Fluid extract: ½ to 1 drachm.

VALERIAN (Valeriana official) is aromatic, stimulant, tonic, anodyne, antispasmodic, and nervine. Valerian is an excellent nerve tonic—very quieting and soothing. Promotes menstruation—taken hot. Valerian is excellent for children with measles, scarlet fever or restlessness—2 tablespoonfuls 2 or 3 times daily. Good for convulsions in infants and is useful for colic, low fevers, colds, and for gravel in the bladder. Heals an ulcerated stomach, prevents fermentation and gas. The tea is healing when applied to sores and pimples externally—must be taken internally at the same time. Valerian helps to relieve palpitation of the heart. The root should not be boiled.

Glossary

Alterative: Herbs that gradually convert an unhealthy condition of an organ to a healthy one. Gradually facilitating a beneficial change in the body. For example ginseng.

Anodyne: Relieves pain and reduces the sensitivity of the nerves.

Antiperiodic: Prevents the periodic recurrence of attacks of a disease; as in malaria.

Antiseptic: Prevents decay or putrefaction. A substance that inhibits the growth and development of microorganisms without necessarily destroying them.

Antispasmodic: An agent that relieves or prevents involuntary muscle spasms or cramps. For example: chamomile.

Aperients: A mild or gentle laxative. Also called Aperitive.

Aromatic: An herb with a pleasant, fragrant scent and a pungent taste.

Astringent: Causes a local contraction of the skin, blood vessels, and other tissues, thereby arresting the discharge of blood, mucus, etc. Usually used locally as a topical application. The word topical pertains to a certain area of the skin or to a substance that affects only the area to which it is applied.

Carminative: An herb that helps to prevent gas from forming in the intestines, and also assists in expelling it.

Cathartic: Causes evacuation of the bowels. A cathartic may be either mild (laxative) or vigorous (purgative).

Cephalic: Referring to diseases affecting the head and upper part of the body.

Consumption: In the past, tuberculosis was called consumption.

Demulcent: Soothes, protects, and relieves the irritation of inflamed mucous membranes and other surfaces.

Diaphoresis: Copious perspiration, esp. when medically induced.

Diaphoretic: Promotes perspiration, especially profuse perspiration.

Diuretic: Promotes the production and secretion of urine. For example: parsley.

Deobstruent: Removes obstructions by opening the natural passages or pores of the body.

Detergent: An agent that cleanses boils, ulcers, wounds, etc.

Drachm: A unit of weight of ancient Greece

Emmenagogue: An herb that brings on menstruation. For example, chamomile.

Nervine: A substance that induces and promotes labor.

Opthalmicum: A remedy for diseases of the eye.

Stomachic: Herbs that give strength and tone to the stomach, stimulate digestion, and improve the appetite.

Tonic: Herbs that restore and strengthen the entire system. Produces and restores normal tone. A general tonic would be one that braces up the whole system, such as a cold bath.

About the Author

Ricardo Frazer is an African Centered/Black Psychology Diplomate and Associate Professor of Psychology at Atlanta Metropolitan College. He was elected a fellow of the Linnean Society of London in 2003. The Linnean Society is the oldest extant professional biological society. He completed certification training in Psychic, Herbal, and Alternative Healing in 1981, at the Karmu Foundation in Cambridge, Massachusetts.

Printed in Great Britain
by Amazon

73670574R00066